STOP THE
CREDIBILITY
CRISIS

STOP THE
CREDIBILITY
CRISIS

Three Profitable Strategies to Cultivate Trust & Desire in the Expertise Economy

Debbie Jenkins

Contents

Praise for Stop The Credibility Crisis

Rather than 'stop the train I want to get off', Debs encourages us to drive our own train, under our control powering it with disruption, creation and connection.

Dr Emma Williams, aka The Nerd Coach, author of three books for Postdocs, coffee loving physicist, https://ejwsolutions.com/

We live in noisy times. Knowing how to not only stand out, but also have people trust you has never been harder. But also never been easier. Debs Jenkins has made a career out of helping good people package their thoughts in a way that helps them get in front of the right people and deliver the right message to showcase their credibility. **If you aspire to serve more people, this book is required and should be the next book on your reading list. I can certainly vouch for the credibility of the author!**

Callum Laing, Entrepreneur, Investor and client of Debs (because he loves me), https://www.callumlaing.com/

In 'Stop The Credibility Crisis', Debbie Jenkins provides a compelling roadmap for overcoming the common pitfalls that professionals face online. Her focus on **the strategic application of disruption, creation, and connection offers a powerful formula for establishing genuine credibility.** *As someone who has navigated these challenges, I find her advice not only practical but imperative for success.*

Ann Latham, author of *The Disconnect Principle* and *The Power of Clarity*, https://annlatham.com/

From page one of The Credibility Crisis I found myself saying 'that's me!... That's exactly what I think too'. Debs has managed to pull together all the issues which consultants, coaches and 'thought leaders' are facing in today's fast moving environment. The key issue for me is how do I stand out, and in this book you will find yourself stretched and challenged. There are so many models that can help you identify where you need to act: P51 - the scale of disruption, P93 Scale of connection and the 'Desire/Trust' Quadrant".

Elaine Gold, Business Diplomat, https://elaine-gold.com/

This book is a game changer as it pushes and challenges you to think and act differently. No sitting around complaining about what could be, it gives you the insights and tools to actually make it happen. With a simple and straightforward approach, **I finished the book knowing exactly what 3 dials to turn up to move forward, excited to disrupt, create and connect.** Watch out world!

Debra Corey, Chief Pay it Forward Officer at DebCo HR,
https://www.debcohr.com/

I just finished reading Stop the Credibility Crisis by Debbie Jenkins. And yet again, I couldn't put her book down. Aptly titled, she has found a way through the credibility crisis **providing clarity to the challenges of AI, content overload, connection and disruption.** I love that "creation is the currency". It soothes my soul and clarifies my own strategy for how I want to be in this noisy world. It's a book I'll recommend to my own clients as there's nothing better than helping their souls be soothed too. Debbie has become her own greatest experiment proving her worth by living what she writes. Already, I'm on the waiting list for her next book. What better tribute to her valuable work!

Finola Howard, Marketing Strategist and Thinking Partner, author of *What If?,*
https://www.finolahoward.com

WARNING: DANGER OF HIGH DENSITY!

This isn't just a book; it's a workout for your brain and business. While reading can fill your head with wonderful ideas, it's the doing that truly transforms. That's precisely why this book doesn't come alone; it's armed with an arsenal of additional materials designed to catapult you from passive page-turning to dynamic action-taking. You can get access by scanning the QR Code or going straight over to www.thecredibilitycrisis.com

Prologue

"I have to start again, again!"

This phrase has become a familiar refrain in my life. You could say I've become adept at what the business world fondly calls "pivots". Change is a constant companion, and adapting to it has become second nature to me.

One of the most significant pivots was when I decided to sell my share in the business I had co-founded. I often half-jokingly say that the business truly flourished after I left – and the truth is, it really did. But that decision meant I was back to square one. I left behind not just a business but the relationships, connections and assets I had nurtured and created over the previous fifteen years. And that wasn't the only restart I faced.

Around the same time, I also ended a twenty-year marriage that from the outside seemed perfect, said goodbye to a couple of houses, a boat and… importantly, waved off the deep-seated loneliness that had lingered like an uninvited guest. It was a parting of ways that felt overdue, leaving space for newfound freedom and clarity.

The third pivot, equally momentous, was a shift in my own mindset. I went on a journey of self-discovery,[1] re-evaluating what truly mattered to me, and who I wanted to be when I grew up. This wasn't just about changing scenery or partners; it was a profound transformation in how I viewed myself and my place in the world. It was about finding clarity in the chaos and redefining success on my own terms. It's when I realised I had a credibility crisis, and it was my own fault.

I've relearnt how to be daring. How about you?

---

1. Not the navel-gazing, Indian yoga retreat style.

The problem

If you've started (or continued) a consulting, training or coaching business (expertise-based businesses) in the last ten years you have survived through one of the most chaotic and disruptive periods in business history.[1] The past two decades haven't just been eventful; there's been a seismic shift in the business landscape.[2]

Think about it: social media and smartphones haven't just entered the market; they've taken over. The sharing economy, remote work and blockchain aren't just buzzwords; they're the new normal, rewriting the rules as we know them. And e-commerce? It's not a fancy add-on anymore; it's more essential than having a business card.

But it's not just about technology. The global focus on mental health and environmental sustainability is growing louder and more insistent. Business coaches who don't have a specific speciality might find that they have clients with mental health issues, that need to be referred to qualified practitioners that are few in number. These aren't gentle ripples of change; they're tidal waves, reshaping the very bedrock of traditional business models. Today's clients don't just want products or services; they demand convenience, transparency and values that align with their own. That's what you want, right?

The line between our professional and personal lives? That's become a relic of the past. We are always connected, and if we're not careful, always accessible. And let's not forget AI and automation. They're transforming the landscape, offering unprecedented efficiency but also raising serious questions about data security and job stability.

This relentless wave of change directly feeds into the Credibility Crisis facing expertise-based business owners today. In an era where every Tom, Dick and Harriette claim to be a guru atop their digital mountain, standing out as a credible, trustworthy expert is tougher than ever. Clients, overwhelmed by options and wary of empty promises, are scrutinising not just what you offer, but who you are and what you stand for. **It's no longer enough to simply be good at what you do. Growing and maintaining credibility is not just a nice-to-have; it's the cornerstone of survival and success.** Your response to these changes, your adaptation and your innovation are the flags you raise to signal your expertise and integrity in this uncertainty.

Right now, you might feel like you're standing on shifting, quaking ground. Every step feels tentative, each decision more critical than the last. It's as if the earth beneath your feet is constantly moving, reshaping, and leaving you in a perpetual state of imbalance.[3] This feeling, though unnerving, is not just normal; it's the hallmark of our times. The true challenge is to find your footing, to create your own solid ground amidst the tumult of change.

Understanding the Expertise Economy

The expertise economy is all about the *value* of what you know. Specialised knowledge and skills are the main drivers of economic growth, making experts (consultants, coaches, authors) very important. This means if you're really good at something, your expertise can open doors to new opportunities and success. Unlike older economies that focused on making and selling physical products, the expertise economy focuses on ideas, innovation and solving complex problems. It's a derivative of Drucker's "knowledge economy"[4] where, deep knowledge in a specific area can make you stand out and become more valuable to businesses and clients. Developing and leveraging deep, specialised skills to solve complex problems leads to thought leadership and niche consulting opportunities.

The problem is the world we live in

The expertise economy is rapidly changing, with digital transformation disrupting traditional business models. We're seeing new platforms, online coaching services and AI-driven solutions challenging the old ways. As a consultant, I've noticed an increasing number of competitors entering the market, offering similar services, often at lower rates.[5] This saturation is making it difficult to stand out and gain clients.

Your dream outcome would be to establish yourself as an authority in your niche, and leverage your expertise to drive consistent business, with clients actively seeking you out. Sounds perfect, right?

But various market forces are making it increasingly difficult to demonstrate credibility. Here are a few significant ones:

1. **Information overload**: The sheer volume of information available online has led to a noisy marketplace where every individual or business is vying for attention. This makes it **harder to cut through the noise and demonstrate you are the signal!** Not only that, potential clients often feel they can find the answers themselves, making them reluctant to invest in professional services.

2. **Competition**: With the internet breaking down geographical barriers, competition is now global. This means you're not just competing with local businesses but also those across the world. **It's increasingly hard to articulate what sets you apart from others.** You need a way to convey your unique value proposition clearly and compellingly.

3. **Rapid technological change**: Our skills or knowledge can become obsolete. Remember when you needed a library card to get access to encyclopaedic knowledge, and you had to understand the Dewey Decimal system to find the right book? Now you can get out-of-date information in moments.[6]

4. **Fake news and disinformation**: In recent years, there's been a surge in the spread of false information, leading to an overall increase in scepticism and mistrust. This impacts the credibility of all sources, particularly online with the increase in information hallucinated by AI.

5. **Social media**: Social media influencers with large followings can shape public opinion, whether their insights are based on expertise or not. This can create a challenging environment for truly credible sources to get heard.

6. **Review culture**: Online reviews can significantly influence a brand or individual's credibility. Negative reviews, even if they are unfair or based on misunderstanding, can damage credibility.

7. **Crisis of trust**: There's an overall decline in trust towards institutions (governments seen as self-serving), media (news outlets accused of bias) and businesses (companies prioritising profits over ethics). This ad-spectrum credibility crisis makes it more difficult for anyone trying to establish trust and authenticity. In fact the very tactics to increase trust (sharing of information) brings us right round to problem one on the list – information overload.

The big question then: **How do expertise-based business owners not just survive but thrive in this whirlwind of change?** How do we turn these challenges into opportunities for innovation and growth?

The thing is, the standard playbook of advice we're getting is probably wrong. It's not for us and it's not for now.

- We are not newbie start-ups or apprentices – we have years of experience, qualifications and training.

- We are not freelancers or jobbers – our solutions are not fungible commodities that can be interchanged.

- We are not faceless corporations – our structure is flexible and personalised, where clients have the privilege of direct interaction with the decision-makers, the CEOs.

We are experts, consultants, thought leaders, owners of expert-led businesses.

In the following diagram, replace the word "consultant" with your "title". Whether you're a coach, trainer, speaker, founder, author or all of the above, the asset path framework will help you think of your ascension.

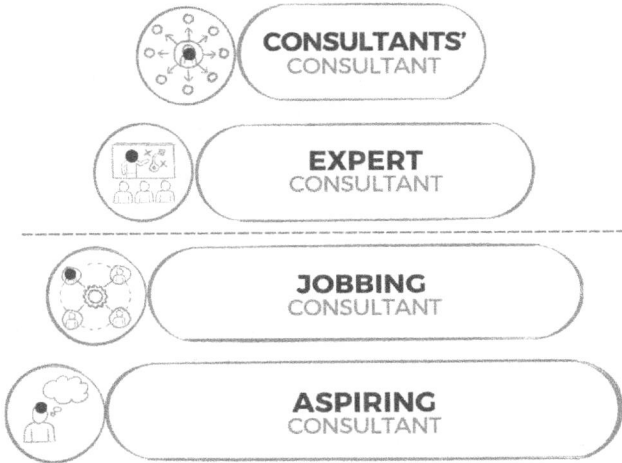

We have graduated from **Aspiring Consultants** at the bottom of the pyramid. We can promote ourselves from the apprentice role. We don't *need* to keep getting the qualifications. Of course, continual learning plays a part, but *we are enough*.

We have delivered other people's intellectual property, shared their models, trained on their frameworks, helped *them* grow *their* businesses. We don't need to carry on as **Jobbing Consultants**: we have paid our jobbing dues – with our time.

Below that dotted line is the danger zone, there are a lot of people down there. The price you can charge is dictated by the market, you are compared to others, you are a commodity. It's difficult to stand out and get selected, there's no barrier to entry. It's a noisy, shouty place full of AI-enabled wannabees. You want to get above the line as soon as possible. And stay above the line.

We are **Expert Consultants**: we've earnt the expert status. Our businesses are viable, we've created assets, curated a network of connections, we've disrupted industries and categories. It's time to capitalise on our IP, what I prefer to think of as intellectual perspective[7], and claim the **Consultants' Consultant** top slot, because nobody will give it to you.

> What are business assets? These are the manifestations and realisations of your intellectual perspective. We grow our business by transforming ideas into assets. Business assets are not limited to tangible items like property or equipment. Assets include your content and books you've published, websites and apps you've created, the skills and knowledge of you and your team, the relationships and connections you've grown.

It looks like a steady path to success, right? I've been talking about this path for years. It's the path I'm on, the path I show my clients.

But it isn't enough, because just when we start to feel sure of our expert status and ready to take that top slot we hit the credibility crisis. We have new problems of:

1. **Maintaining authority**: Once you've established yourself, there's the constant pressure to stay ahead, continue learning and maintain status. The last thing you want is to become complacent and lose your edge.

2. **Scaling challenges**: With increased demand, managing time and resources becomes critical. How do you ensure that the quality of your services remains consistent as your business grows? How do you ensure the demand keeps coming? How do you keep creating assets, products and services the market wants?

3. **Adapting to change**: It's not going to stop changing. Staying adaptable and receptive to new methodologies and technologies is vital to remain relevant. The world is changing and you need to change too.

The problem is us. We're looking for stability in an unstable world. We're hoping to sell the big-ticket coaching gigs without creating a connection. We're waiting for answers from people who know less than we do. If you can't differentiate yourself, you risk fading into obscurity, losing potential business. There's a constant hustle. But it's not our fault (well, it's not my fault, I can't speak for you!)

The problem is you, me, us (but it's not our fault)

Once upon a time, we could shield our work with impressive barriers – peer-reviewed research papers, books vetted, published and promoted by discerning publishers, keynote speeches that sparked conversations and set standards. But those barriers? They've been systematically dismantled in the content-sharing age. The first bricks were chipped away by the advent of the internet, social media bulldozed through a few more, and now, AI has obliterated what was left of the wall.

The digital era, especially the past two decades, has democratised information access and sharing. This democratisation meant that anyone with an internet connection could claim expertise. The lack of barriers, combined with the human penchant for shortcuts, led many to claim expert status without doing the legwork. The '80s and '90s saw a clear distinction between experts and laypeople. You'd have experts appearing on television, writing books or giving lectures. Today, a viral tweet or a trending LinkedIn post can establish someone as an "expert", regardless of their actual qualifications. And who watches the television? There's no gatekeeper.

How do our potential clients work out who to trust? How do they know that the thing they think they want will even work?

This is what it feels like to be your potential client or customer.

You know this is true, because sometimes you are on the right hand side of the line.

So, what's the game plan now? Do we stop innovating, stop leading with our thoughts? Do we sit back and watch as our expertise and years of experience are undermined? Absolutely not. The game has changed, and so must our strategies. We need to redefine what it means to be a thought leader and expert in this uncharted territory.

In product design, there's a saying: "Faster? Cheaper? Better? Pick two." We've fallen into the trap of trying to do all three. Which means we're not faster, cheaper or better, and it's become a speedy way to exhaustion.

We can blame the rest of the world, fake qualifications, over-hyped marketing. Or we can take it on the chin, and realise we're probably our own worst enemies.

Some of the main issues when establishing credibility:

1. **Lack of consistency**: Credibility is established over time through consistent actions and behaviours. Inconsistencies in actions, message or branding can erode credibility quickly. I know you've *started* posting on LinkedIn, sending a newsletter or writing a book. But are you consistent? Have you bounced from idea to new fad and back again? Me too. Let's address this in the Disruption and Synthesis chapters.

2. **Over-promising and under-delivering**: Making grandiose claims or promises that aren't fulfilled can severely damage credibility. It's always better to under-promise and over-deliver than the other way around. I've been saying this for the last twenty-seven years, and I still forget.[8] The Bro Comms bros with their over the top communications style have

over-promising down to an art; bragging is second nature. We'll hear more about them in the next chapter. You can solve this by creating systems.

3. **Lack of transparency**: Transparency fosters trust. In contrast, a lack of transparency or openness about mistakes, shortcomings or changes can make it hard to appear credible. This doesn't mean we go around airing our dirty washing in public; it means we connect with real people because we are real people. Find out how in the Connection chapters.

4. **Impersonality or lack of authenticity**: People trust and connect with other people, not faceless entities. If you or your brand lacks a human touch, personal story or genuine voice, establishing credibility becomes more difficult. The royal we isn't helping you; the hands off "talk to my assistant" doesn't make you sound cool (it never did). Find out how to find the right balance in the Synthesis chapters.

5. **Low quality creation, products and presentation**: The quality of your work, your products or even your online content speaks volumes about your credibility. Poorly made products, sloppy work or badly written content can all undermine credibility. And it's really not acceptable. Fourteen-year olds can turn out high quality content. Read more in the Creation section.

6. **Ignoring feedback**: Part of being credible is showing that you're open to feedback and willing to make changes when necessary. Ignoring criticism or

feedback can make it appear as though you don't respect or value others' opinions. Get into a positive creation cycle of listen, launch, learn, loop which we'll look at in the Creation section.

7. **No evidence of success**: Case studies, testimonials and proven results can help to establish your credibility. Without these, it's much harder to prove that you're capable of delivering what you promise. You need to drop credibility clues. We'll talk about these in the Creation section.

You're causing your own credibility crisis. I know, I'm doing it too!

Overcoming these issues requires careful planning, genuine effort and patience. Credibility can't be built overnight, but it's one of the most valuable assets any individual can have.

If the problem is us, not the rest of the world, then we have agency, power and response-ability.

Your credibility crisis
...You have control over:

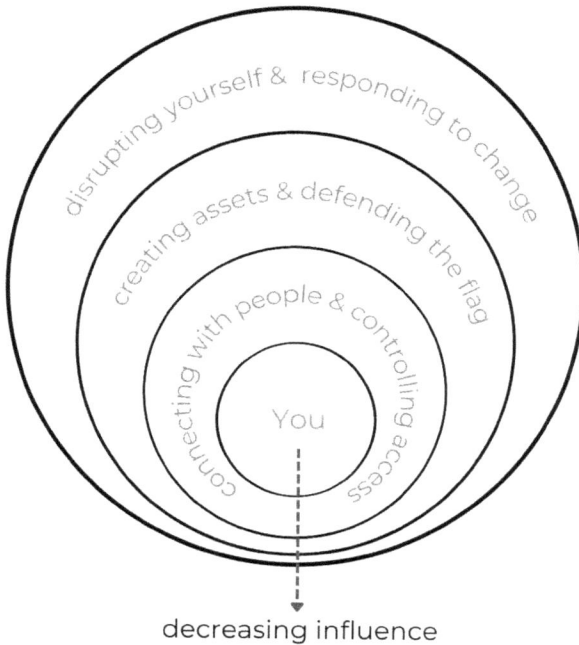

disrupting yourself & responding to change

creating assets & defending the flag

connecting with people & controlling access

You

decreasing influence

We are in the inner circle. We have *control* over ourselves, the actions we take, the decisions we make. The outer circles are the where we have decreasing influence. We cannot control how other people see us, we only have *influence* over perception, other people and the AI bots.

That's all great and logical, but we're human beings with feelings, cares, concerns and bills to pay. It's not just about the facts, it's about how it makes us feel – exhausted, scared, overwhelmed. If we're of a certain age we might even be hoping things slow down just long enough for us to make it to the end and finish topping up our pensions.[9]

For me, it feels like a daily race through the Kubler-Ross grief stages:[10]

1. Denial – really, ChatGPT can write a book?

2. Anger – you're joking, first everyone who wrote a book became a book coach, and now everyone is a book coach because they have their little AI helper.

3. Bargaining – yes, but ... it won't have the nuance, the sarcasm, the depth, the experience, the models.

4. Depression – what? You can train it to be sarcastic, just like me? You can teach it about your own models? Really?

5. Acceptance – OK, so what do I do now?

And of course, I don't do this in order, moving from one stage to the other. I'll jump around, getting myself an extra bit of depression on a Monday! I also don't do this for just one subject. You might have your own complaints about your industry or area: Really, AI therapists? Twenty-year old life coaches? She got a publishing deal – what does she know about negotiating?

These are strong feelings.

You may, like me, have found yourself

- wrestling with the relentless pace of change (can it just pause for a day?)

- searching for certainty in your next steps (someone, please just tell me what to do)

- looking for courage to make decisions that impact your clients, employees and your family (all those livelihoods I can impact).

Know that you're not alone.

It's a common feeling, especially when the ground beneath us seems to be constantly shifting. This search for certainty isn't just about finding stability; it's about creating a place for ourselves where we can stand firm, confident in our direction and decisions.

We're really striving for a sense of fulfilment. To achieve a status that gets respect from our peers – a recognition of our expertise and contributions. It's about carving out a niche where we are valued and respected. We want the freedom to make choices about what we do, who we do it for and when we do it. We need to align our professional life with our personal values, giving us a sense of control and purpose in a world that often feels unpredictable.

But it's not about standing alone. We yearn for relatedness, a connection to a cause greater than ourselves and to a community that shares our values and vision. This sense of belonging and shared purpose is what drives us forward, what keeps us anchored amidst chaos. And lastly, we seek fairness – an even playing field where opportunities are accessible, where our efforts and talents are recognised and rewarded appropriately.

Understanding our own desires helps us transform our frustration into focused action, and as you'll see in the final part of the book, helps us better understand the people we want to work with. It guides us in charting a course that not only brings us personal satisfaction and success but also contributes positively to the community and the field we are passionate about, growing trust in our abilities.

Look, I know you've worked hard, had your failures, tried things and screwed them up, fought back and learnt. Your education and experiences, knowledge and capabilities, have brought you here. Now it smarts (well actually pisses me off) when a client says they'll use AI because it's faster. Or you lose out to an inexperienced newcomer. This is the credibility crisis. So, what's the antidote?

---

1. Daniel Priestley in Entrepreneur: 10 Business Trends That Defined the 2010s https://entm.ag/8y71

2. James Manyika and Monique Tuin in McKinsey Global Institute, It's time to build 21st century companies: Learning to thrive in a radically different world:https://www.mckinsey.com/mgi/overview/in-the-news/its-time-to-build-21st-century-companies

3. And it's not just the menopause, though I do blame the menopause for most of my problems.

4. Drucker, Peter. "The term 'knowledge economy'." *FourWeekMBA*. https://fourweekmba.com/knowledge economy/

5. This is nothing new, it's been a problem since the stallholders in Mesopotamia in 3200 BCE claimed, "My pots are infused with the essence of the Tigris itself, and for fewer sheaves of wheat than my esteemed competitor!"

6. It's possible that the outdated books were specific to our local library, given the "economically challenged" area I grew up in. Back in the 1970s, to access more current resources, we would take two bus rides to reach the central city library.

7. IP usually means intellectual property; creations of your mind such as inventions, designs, symbols, that are protected by law through copyright, patents and trademarks. Sometimes we haven't protected our ideas (though we should, see the creation chapter) and I consider those intellectual *perspectives*, equally valuable to the user, and worth sharing.

8. Though do remember to make it clear that you gave more or faster than expected, otherwise it becomes an expectation and not a bonus.

9. Maybe that's just me?

10. Kübler-Ross, E. *On Death and Dying*. 1969. New York, NY: Macmillan. Introduced the five stages of grief, commonly referred to as the Kübler-Ross model, which includes denial, anger, bargaining, depression, and acceptance.

The antidote?

It was a simple time, the late 1900s. You'd meet people face to face. Get qualified to prove your knowledge. Print out your business cards and set yourself up as an expert consultant, coach or trainer. Get your dozen music CDs for 1p delivered by mail to your house,[1] and go to your local business chamber to swap those business cards (they were doing no good in your desk drawer).

Then the internet happened, with an explosion of information, streaming music and online competitors. The erosion of trust accelerated as advances in technology created utterly believable lies and digital deceptions, blurring the lines between fact and fiction, and challenging our ability to discern truth in a sea of manipulated realities.

We can't go back to that simpler world.

The antidote to the credibility crisis comes down to three strategies, or dials that you can turn up and down:

1. **Disruption is the catalyst** – that helps you be seen and heard. Challenge the norms, defy conventional thinking, and disrupt the status quo with bold ideas, unconventional communication and fearless innovation.

2. **Creation is the currency** – that is exchanged for your potential client's time. Show your expertise through writing a series of transformative books, creating innovative content, developing engaging programs and events, being featured in industry-leading journals, and delivering powerful speeches.

3. **Connection is the cure** – to impersonality, overwhelm and isolation. Cultivate one-to-one connections, personal interactions and direct engagement through live events, coaching sessions and interactive platforms.

I'm going to show you how these concepts play out in the rest of the book, and how we can synthesise the ideas to avoid the credibility crisis.

Confusion is caused because there are too many people guruing[2] about selling false antidotes.

The false antidotes:

1. **Ego-driven content –** the age-old trap of creating content for self-aggrandisement rather than genuine value. Regularly publishing self-promotional content that lacks depth, substance or any bloody value. Then doing it again. Then doing it some more. It's like shouting into a void, hoping someone hears how great you think you are.

2. **Echo chamber engagement –** people engaging solely within their comfort zone, listening only to voices that mirror their own. Missing out on broader

perspectives and growth as they wine and whine over their Chardonnay. It's a recipe for stagnation, not innovation.

3. **Excess-driven growth** – pursuing growth for growth's sake, without purpose or direction. Like trying to fill a bucket with a massive hole at the bottom – it's never-ending and never-fulfilling. Your 7 figure gurus, the 2 comma clubbers and the Bro Comms bros are leading everyone astray.[3]

Watching back-to-back *Diary of a CEO* when you're navigating through a rough patch in your established business is like drinking *Quarta Caffè* espresso to calm your nerves.[4,5] It's fascinating and invigorating, yet you end up even more restless and stressed, comparing your journey to a unicorn's trajectory.

You might be pushing back at me too, with your brilliant reasons why overcoming the credibility crisis isn't important:

1. **"I don't have time."** I know you're busy. Addressing the credibility crisis takes time and effort, and you might feel overwhelmed. But it isn't going away and it won't get any easier than today.

2. **"I've been doing this for years without focusing on credibility."** I know your experience and past success speak for themselves. But if nobody is listening, or they can't hear you over the noise, they will never hear how great you are.

3. **"I'm already successful. Why do I need to change?"**
   Maybe you don't. Perhaps the risk of change is higher
   than the risk of staying the same. Or maybe AI will eat
   your breakfast.

4. **"Credibility is built over time. I can't speed it
   up."** Yes, it is built over time. It's also eroded over
   time. Complacency is the fastest way to lose your
   connections and mind share. It's not a passive sport.

5. **"I'm not comfortable exposing myself."** I know
   it's scary to talk about vulnerabilities and failures;
   some people will be repelled. It's also scary to talk
   about successes. Vulnerability is your most potent
   weapon against the credibility crisis. Your failures *and*
   successes leave footprints for others to follow.

Overcoming the credibility crisis often requires stepping out
of your comfort zone. I'm going to make this as easy as
possible, encouraging you to do the things you already do
but more and better.

The credibility matrix – the dynamics of trust and desire

Let's put some dimensions on the credibility crisis so we can
measure, improve and repeat.

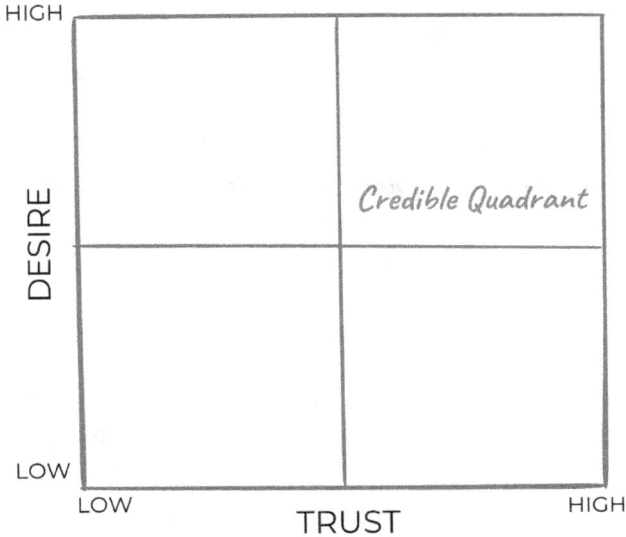

In the heart of the credibility crisis is the balance between two age-old human dimensions: trust and desire. These are the fundamental measures by which we have always judged leaders, movements and messages, from the ancient classics through world religions to modern politics. Do I trust this person? Do I want what they're selling?[6]

What is credibility? I believe it's the communication of desirable value and trustworthiness.

The credibility matrix puts these dimensions into a measurable framework that helps us analyse, enhance and replicate credibility in any context. Trust is the foundation – the bedrock of belief in someone's reliability, ethics and integrity. This is the solid ground. Without trust, no amount of desire can build a lasting bridge between you and your audience.

There's a lot of psychology backing up the ideas in this book. I'm a bit of a nerd, I've even published some authors discussing these subjects. If you want a short primer get a copy of **The Expert Edge: Unlocking the Psychology of Credibility** by signing up at www.thecredibilitycrisis.com

But, trust can be eroded and faked.

Desire, on the other hand, is the magnetic pull. It is the ability to align what you offer – be it a product, a philosophy or a promise – with the desires of the audience. Desire without trust may capture attention momentarily, but it won't secure enduring allegiance.

And, desire can be fabricated and exaggerated.

Credibility can be assessed through the lens of these two aspects. The epics of Homer, the parables of Jesus and the orations of Cicero[7], each in their own way, manipulated trust and desire to inspire, persuade and to get people to move.

In practical terms, the credibility matrix allows us to plot where an individual, a brand, a product, a book or an institution stands. Do they evoke trust but fail to ignite desire? Boring, same old offers, lacking in creativity. Or do they inspire desire yet stir scepticism instead of trust? What I'm cheekily calling Bro Comms, I'll explain more later. To achieve credibility we need to be trustworthy *and* resonate with the intrinsic motivations of the people we want to work with and influence.

Right now, plot yourself on the matrix. Do it quickly without overthinking.

> If you want to see some examples of products, people and institutions plotted on the matrix (from my jaded perspective) come over to www.thecredibilitycrisis.com where you can also download a template.

When I did this in 2022, I put myself down in the bottom right corner. I was a safe pair of hands, that nobody was buying. Boring. I had to do something disruptive to break out of that trap.

Next we'll see how you can turn the three dials of disruption, creation and connection to increase your trust and desirability. These are the three profitable strategies. Then finally we'll look at the trust/desire paradox that makes the credibility crisis so much fun! As we are refining what we must do to grow credibility, communicate desire and trustworthiness we can also hone in on what it really means to disrupt, create and connect.

How to think about this book: It's not a how to, I'm not giving you a list of answers and actions to fix your own or *the* credibility crisis. I don't have the directions to give you. It's not a map. I certainly haven't covered all the terrain, the nooks and crannies, the nuances and niches. This is my attempt at a warning – a lighthouse, a landmark. A shout out to get you thinking about the problems and the chaos they bring, in an ordered way. It's a look at the view of the valleys from halfway up a mountain. I'm waving a flag – a warning flag – that things are changing and you need to look up.

This is my first "serious" book, which is why I have doubled down on the humour (for humour, read sarcasm). You'll usually find me writing books about how to get things done. How to write a book (my day job), how to sell a book (don't), how to make paella (I live in Spain), how to market your business (add value). I'm comfortable in the "how to", what I call directions type books. Sometimes getting stuck in the how to means you don't look up long enough to see the why to. That's what this book is all about. As you read, ask yourself, "Why?"

---

1. Twelve hot hits for a penny from Columbia Records. I think I still owe them a few hundred quid!

2. Shout out to my first (even though he didn't know it at the time) mentor, Geoff Burch, who does a brilliant skit about guruing! Read any of his books for a giggle.

3. No disrespect to bros, but you know what I mean: the Ferrari, the wad of cash, the fast-speaking in your face "buy it now or it's gone forever" type of communication.

4. My partner's Italian. We get yearly food parcels of *Quarta Caffè* and delicious Italian sweets. The one thing I'll run up the food miles for!

5. *The Diary of a CEO* with Steven Bartlett – https://stevenbartlett.com/the-diary-of-a-ceo-podcast

6. I'd argue that religions and governments are two of the most capitalist institutions. Both seek to 'market' their ideologies and policies, striving to generate 'buy-in' from the public. As Adam Smith said in *An Inquiry into the Nature & Causes of the Wealth of Nations, Vol 1*: "It is not from the benevolence of the butcher, the brewer, or the baker that we expect our dinner, but from their regard to their own self-interest."

7. Look at me sounding all grown up and well-read!

PART 1: DISRUPTION

Disruption is the catalyst

I'm going to start with disruption (even though later you'll see why disruption should come last) because disruption is where we end up at 4 a.m. in our overworked minds, panicking that we've seen yet another competitor get a great deal that should have been ours.[1] Or pissed off because a less experienced consultant got an impressive book deal or mention in Forbes. Or, secretly and with a sense of shame, rewriting the words for our website with the help of ChatGPT, knowing that we're just rearranging the deckchairs on the Titanic.

We are in an age of disruption, it started with the wheel and will end with the robots taking over the world.

What does it even mean to disrupt? Disrupt what exactly? Disrupt for disruptions' sake? After a while the word doesn't even make sense, right? Can you call yourself disruptive?

The problem with the credibility crisis is that unless we do something different we are compared with everyone else. And clients don't know how to make a fair comparison.

Nobody buys coaching.

Nobody buys consultancy.

Nobody buys books.

People buy transformation.

To get a transformation something has to change – that's the disruption. Disruption causes a choice, the potential client can stay the same or do something different. Better or more causes a comparison with all the other coaches and consultants out there.

It's not you inventing a category or finding your purpose or turning the swearing up to 11.[2] Though all of those things might help *you* feel good and get attention, they won't necessarily help the client.

The disruption you're looking for is for your one special client, the one person whose life you can change by solving their most important problem. It's your one way of delivering it that is hugely desirable and transformative. It's who you are that leads them to make a change and get their transformation.

- Disrupt by who you are: dangerous, daring, outrageous, contrary, intuitive, wise, empathetic, bold.

- Disrupt by what you do: hosting immersive workshops, executing guerrilla marketing campaigns, crafting viral storytelling, organising hackathons, create No Summit Summits[3] or conducting interactive webinars.

- Disrupt by how you do it: leveraging novel techniques, embracing agile methodologies, integrating cross-disciplinary insights, adopting a user-centric design, or pioneering innovative concepts.

- Disrupt by who you do it for and with: targeting special people within niche markets, focusing on selective audiences who appreciate you, maintaining exclusivity or engaging with a highly focused group.

- Disrupt by what you give them: achieving clarity in strategy, measurable results, significant progress, a sense of empowerment and breakthrough, intimate experiences.

- Disrupt by why you do what you do: to challenge the status quo, to empower the under-represented, to democratise knowledge, to inspire change, to foster community, to bridge divides, to ignite creativity, to advance sustainability, to amplify voices.

> Get your copy of the Desirable Disruption Matrix over at www.thecredibilitycrisis.com

You can see how by disrupting in any one of these categories you will stand out and be more desirable.

Take five minutes to note where you might easily be disruptive.

Having twenty years of repeating the same year's experience doesn't equate to twenty years of growing experience; it's merely a single year of learning, lived twenty times over. Yes, you might be an expert at making that cheese toastie because you've made it every day for the last twenty years, but you won't be getting a Michelin star any time soon. You're not disruptive if you've had the same year of experience for the last twenty years. That's why the newcomers with two years of experience are eating your lunch, and why the robots seem so threatening.

You might be thinking: "Despite writing books and giving talks, it feels like my message isn't cutting through. I'm looking for a transformation in how the market perceives me. I don't want to be just another consultant; I want to be seen as a trusted, authoritative voice in my field. I want my ideas to resonate, to spark discussions, to influence decisions. I want to break through the noise, reach more people and truly make an impact."

It's easy to blame the apparent newcomer just jumping out of the jobbing level and claiming the expert slot. But they might just be more expert than me in what my client needs. **That's my credibility crisis**. I can do something about it; it's in my sphere of control. We can relax, because there's plenty for us to do to prove the depth of our experience, ramp up the desirability and make lasting connections.

Don't disrupt for disruption's sake. Disrupt to add value.

Chaos is a feature

I'm a proponent of chaos. I think it's a necessary feature in our lives, and that without it we wouldn't grow. I accept necessary chaos. However, living and working in chaos all the time is not sustainable. We need to find our way around the chaos. We do that with constraints as we'll see soon, but first let's stay in chaos for a moment more.

Our business environment might feel chaotic, but we and our clients are looking for solid ground. Chaos is our crisis mode, and I'll show you why we need to respond. We can't sustain it for long without stress and overwhelm.

The people we are working with, these individuals, organisations, companies, governments, charities, have their own environment. They might be in any of the domains that Dave Snowden identified in the the Cynefin framework.[4] Chaos is only one!

When Dave (I can call him Dave, because that's his name) came up with the model in 1999 we didn't have social media, AI on our laptops and robots cleaning our floors. Mr Beast was celebrating his first birthday.[5] Even today, Dave's model still helps us make sense of an uncertain world, help leaders understand the context of their challenges, offers a structured approach to decision-making, encourages continuous learning and adaptation. It's a useful framework for us and for our clients.

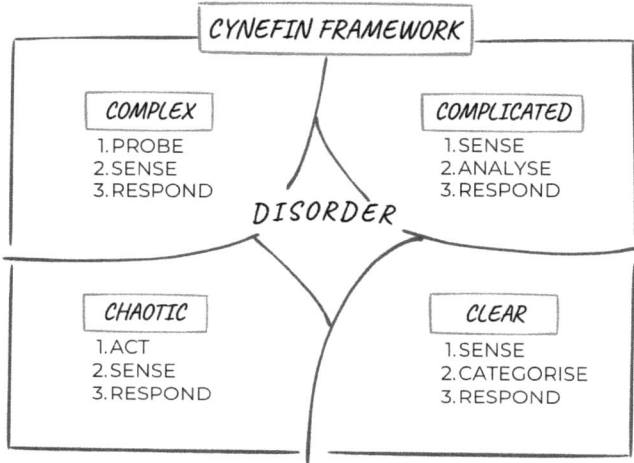

Here's a brief overview of each domain:

- Clear: Best practices. Things are predictable and the relationship between cause and effect is obvious. Everyone can see the right answer. It's like following a recipe.

- Complicated: Expert knowledge. The relationship between cause and effect exists but is not immediately apparent to everyone. It's like assembling a complex piece of machinery. It's about finding the right expert and applying good practices.

- Complex: The relationship between cause and effect can only be perceived in retrospect. It's like raising a child; there are no hard and fast rules. For businesses in complex environments, it's about experimentation and learning by doing.

- Chaotic: This is a crisis mode, where there is no clear relationship between cause and effect. Quick, decisive action is needed to establish order. It's like putting out a fire.

- Disorder: Right in the centre. This is the state of not knowing which of the other four domains applies. It's a state of confusion that requires breaking things down to get better understanding before you can even begin to start.

When you can identify the domain you are in you can make better decisions, take action and move. The problem is as expertise-based business owners we've got used to being in clear, complicated or complex domains, where our expertise leads the way. Traditional marketing consultants embraced social media, and now AI-driven content, comments and connections are flooding the market. Business consultants had frameworks and methodologies for success, and now those processes seem antiquated.

Right now I believe we're in the chaotic domain. Why? Because we are frequently navigating the impacts of sudden AI advancements or automation shifts that leave companies scrambling. New AI tools disrupt industries overnight, and we're expected to apply our expertise to guide strategy without prior models to lean on. We learn to filter noise from signal to make rapid, informed decisions in scenarios without precedent. Seriously, who really believed we'd be outsourcing mental health to AI chatbots?[6]

If we're in the chaotic domain we must ACT first.

And, to be honest, I prefer to be in chaos than in the scary disorder domain – I like taking action, seeing what happens, then responding to the feedback (we'll see in the creation chapter a model for quickly creating assets in a chaotic domain). But, we need to speed up the decision-making to put out the credibility crisis fires.

Jordan Peterson, in his lecture series, *Discovering Personality*, said: *"You can't plan a complex[7] system because the assumptions that you're making while you're making your plans are going to change on you in an unexpected way."[8]*

This is why plans are useless and planning is everything. By the time you've written your plan, shared it with your team, and come up with the catchy slogan, things have changed. No plan survives contact with the external environment for expertise based businesses. We need to be in a constant state of vigilance to respond rapidly.

We need to get good at making fast decisions and taking action. But how do we do that when there are so many options and the domain is chaotic? Dan Kowalski, says that under the right circumstance we usually make the right choice, but we don't always get the right circumstances. He provides a series of flow charts to help you make Weighed, Informed, Sufficient, Effective choices under challenging circumstances: "We make decisions all the time. Not all count as W.I.S.E. choices, but often this is because we don't have time to think thoroughly. If you can take just five minutes, you can assess any decision."[9]

You've got five minutes. In the chaotic domain we need to regularly make those five minute blocks to learn (ask for feedback, monitor stats, check the horizon) and adjust (decide to launch something new, implement findings, connect with relevant people).

But we're not wired for making 'good' decisions. Warren Buffett's right-hand man at Berkshire Hathaway, Charlie Munger, wrote a comprehensive analysis of the various psychological tendencies that lead people to make errors in judgement and decision-making; "Psychology of Human Misjudgment".[10] When we're making changes and challenging ourselves to make a difference we're in a chaotic business environment (pretty much all the time, right?). That's when the errors come faster and more frequently. Munger, first presented these ideas in a famous lecture at Harvard University in 1995. One of the "25 Tendencies" he shared was the "Deprival-Superreaction Tendency" because people often react more intensely to a threat of losing something (pain) than to the prospect of gaining something of equal value. That's why Bro Comms marketers focus on pain when they're trying to influence you and why you desperately want to go to the local swimming pool after they've closed it.[11]

If I'm right, and we're in the chaos domain, that means that right now we're deprived of certainty. Things become disproportionately more valuable when we're deprived of them.

The more chaos there is the more we desire stability.

We can use this cognitive bias in our favour too. The fear of losing market position, clients or relevance can be a more powerful motivator than the potential gains from new opportunities. This fear can drive us to innovate and disrupt our own practices before someone else does. Complacency (or apathy) due to a desire to maintain the status quo can lead to a greater loss when inevitable changes in the market occur. We need to be proactive rather than reactive because waiting until disruption is forced upon us often means acting under less favourable conditions.

That's why we need constraints.

Constraints are necessary

Constraints are how we impose structure in our chaotic world. It's how we make sense of things just long enough to make decisions and take action. Without constraints our systems and processes would tend towards decay and entropy. If you don't clean your teeth daily your pearly smile will rot and your teeth will fall out. However, if you clean your teeth one hundred times per day your teeth will not get one hundred times better. The number of times is a useful constraint.

Considering we only have about 4000 weeks in a typical lifetime, time emerges not just as a resource, but as the most fundamental constraint under which we operate.[12] Our challenge, then, is not to 'manage' time but to live and work well within the time we have, because we cannot do everything.[13]

It's easy to get side-tracked and over-excited by the new tech, the fastest AI, the latest LLM.[14] Constraints serve not as barriers, but as clarifying forces that define authenticity and integrity.

The questions we must ask ourselves, to turn on constraints, are: will this serve my customers better? Will this add value to my clients, my business or my team? Is this strategic or shiny?

Constraints can be set upon us and we can set them upon ourselves.

> If you want to get out of the mire of chaos then get a full Chaos to Creation training along with the Chaos to Creation Manifesto. Visit www.TheCredibilityCrisis.com

Constraints help us create solid ground, an anchor point to work from. You're not Lara Croft running, jumping and "huh"-ing from one shifting stone to another. Let's pause and get constraints working for us.

In the *Chaos to Creation Model and Manifesto*, I share a bunch of constraints you can use to keep you on track whether you're creating an asset (see the next section) or growing your business. Here's the list with an example of each:

- Add (introducing a new feature to a product)

- Subtract (removing steps from your business program)

- Multiply (expanding reach by adding partners)

- Divide (segmenting customer base or products)

- Pause (temporarily putting on hold a membership)

- Go (launching a new marketing campaign)

- Stop (killing off a program or keynote)

- Recycle (selling your "sawdust", what you learnt to get you here)

- Upcycle (transforming an old model or framework)

- Due date (setting a firm deadline for a book launch)

- Do date (scheduling the start date for a new partnership)

- Hours (limiting hours to concentrate demand)

- Money (setting a strict budget)

- Resources (allocating fixed resources)

- What's up first (prioritising the first next step)

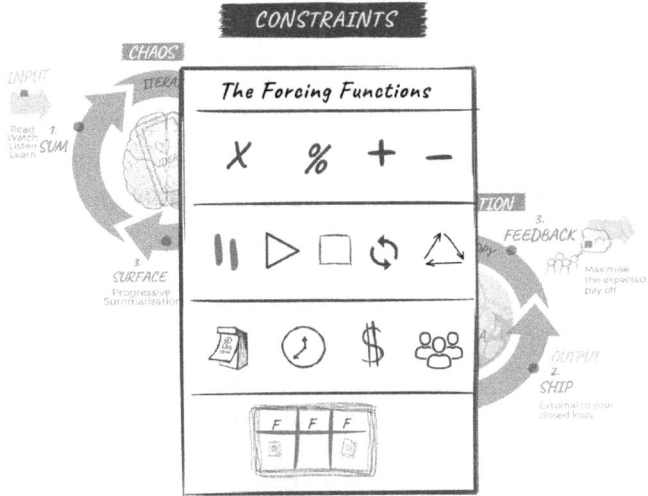

These are the forcing functions of constraints, they stop you from continuing when you should stop, and get you started when you've stalled. You already use constraints and probably don't even think about them. When you set that date for your book launch you also set in motion a cascade of constraints and dependencies. We can use those constraints to create motion in uncertainty.

Because, while you're messing around perfecting something, navel-gazing, learning everything about a subject, someone else is out there creating an asset in the chaos. When you're waiting for approval from your friends, colleagues and mentors for the precise wording on the back cover, someone else has launched an ebook and got that keynote. Set constraints. **Perfection is the enemy.**

To be considered credible we need to be consistent. We thought about this in the opening chapters. As with many ideas in this book, that leads to a paradox. Consistency causes entropy. Entropy causes a lack of desire for what we're doing, creating, selling. Being overly consistent can be a trap. Adapting, evolving and being open to change can enhance credibility, especially now. Emerson said in *Self-Reliance*: "A foolish consistency is the hobgoblin of little minds."[15] **If perfection is the enemy, then consistent perfection is the hobgoblin!**

Stop striving for perfection and start embracing imperfections. The content is more important than the commas. We'll look at this in the next section on creating assets and the Minimum Valuable Asset.

We need to be guided by hysteresis, not hysterics.

Here at the Disaster Farm in Spain we inherited a water tank.[16] It wasn't functional. The previous owner lived here for nineteen years without running water – I don't know how! The water tank holds exactly the same volume as the water delivery truck. Which means when we are getting close to running out of water we have to play an amusing game. If we have too much water we might end up wasting it when the delivery arrives. We have to move fast to get it into the right places. When we need to empty the tank in preparation for a delivery all our trees get an extra dose, the *huerta* (vegetable patch) gets a drowning, buckets and vessels get filled, and the dipping pool gets a top up.

We almost always need a water delivery at the weekend or on a fiesta day – when they won't deliver. So frequently we need to save water for a few days too. When we need to save water I don't do any washing or washing up (oh no!), the plants are on rations, the trees have to wait. We go into pause mode – surviving, rationing, waiting.

Before I lived in the countryside in Spain I was oblivious to the flow of water. I turned on the tap, out it came. Now, I am attuned to our environment, the way we manage our resources and the consequences of lack of oversight. It's the same with ideas:

- Too many ideas and they might get wasted. You might have an overflow (waste) of ideas.

- When you give a little extra attention to your ideas, they blossom.

- We can't fill the ideas water tank ourselves. We need external input to help with the flow.

- We need to use the ideas, not just conserve them.

- Using the ideas creates something new, outside of ourselves, that others can consume. Then we get feedback to bring back into our process.

- It's better to have extra idea space, rather than continually running on empty/full with the associated stress!

I could, of course, really overwork this metaphor – in fact that's one of my super powers (along with getting overexcited by clients' ideas and making naan bread) – so I'll stop now! This is where the creation in constraints ideas hysteresis loop came from. This is my hysteresis loop for ideas – not too full, not too empty.[17] (Not to be confused with my hysterical loop when I don't have any ideas!)

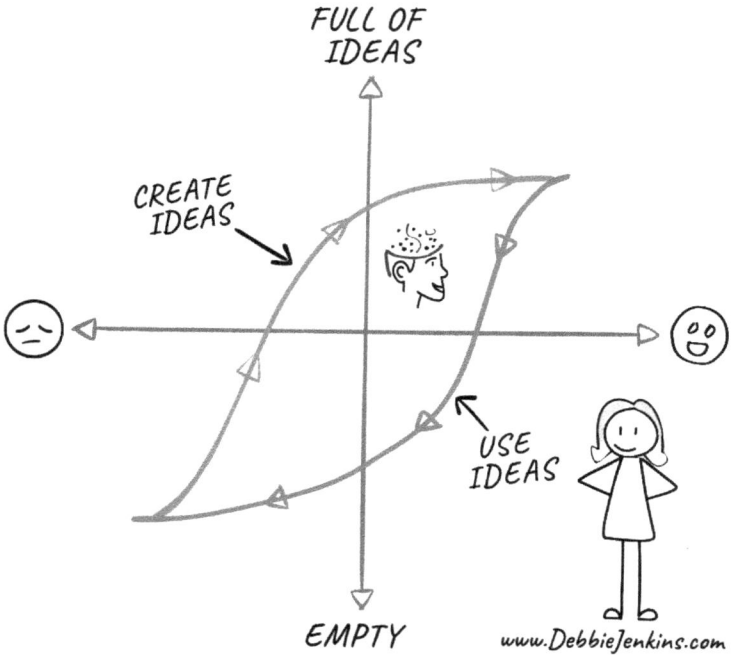

FULL OF IDEAS

CREATE IDEAS

USE IDEAS

EMPTY

www.DebbieJenkins.com

Here are three things to do to keep the ideas (energy) flowing consistently:

1. Trust that more ideas will come – your brain is magic!

2. Use your current ideas, don't save them – make space for new thoughts.

3. Accept that you need external input sometimes – go to conferences, read from outside of your own sphere, get a coach.

Remember, when you turn on that tap to brush your teeth, don't underestimate the flow of your ideas. There's an almost magical way that they come to you, and by sharing them they grow to become something new. Sometimes you might not have ideas... but that's OK. You just need to call the water tank guy for a delivery!

Most expertise-based business owners are ideas rich and time poor. I know you have plenty of ideas. **Your most valuable asset is your time, that is your number one constraint.** So ship those ideas quickly, frequently and with energy. What can you ship today?

When Karen Currier decided to rename the menopause for her book: *DOING intentionally: How to take care of your business through brain fog, anxiety and overwhelm during the menoshift*™, she wasn't doing it to be disruptive deliberately.[18] She had a burning desire to reframe the period of life us women are fortunate to experience.[19] The idea of the "menoshift" took advantage of the constraint of words – a portmanteau that perfectly describes this period of life. Our "menos" aren't "paused", waiting to spring back to life; we've changed, shifted, we embrace and love this period.[20]

Disrupt or be disrupted

When I was pretending to be an electronics engineer over thirty-five years ago I had an epiphany.[21] I started my working life[22] at 16, as a technician (apprenticed to BT), and then worked for Apricot Computers hand designing very complex printed circuit boards (Intel 386 motherboards), way before the software was clever enough to do it all. At nights and weekends for five years I went to university to get my degree (I was a swot. I got a first class electronics degree).

The weird thing was that after the grand graduation ceremony, and even armed with my newfound knowledge and a big certificate, people at work still saw me as a technician. A desk jockey running the million-pound computers to produce more million-pound computers. They didn't see me as an engineer.[23] I had changed, but I was still *used* and *seen* as a technician. They weren't getting the most out of me because of a bias – they "knew" what I could do.

Things change. You change. Your business changes. Bloody hell, everything changes (except Tom Cruise)!

The changes might have happened so slowly you didn't notice. Like traditional brick-and-mortar retail businesses gradually losing market share to online shopping platforms.

Or so fast you didn't understand. The sudden emergence of deepfake technology leading to a credibility crisis in media, politics and personal security.

The changes might have been so quiet you didn't hear them coming. The subtle but pervasive shift in consumer privacy expectations, as people became more accustomed to free digital services, they unknowingly traded their personal data for convenience.

Disruption doesn't have to be seismic to impact you and your business. I talk to my clients about two types of problems they can solve – bleeding neck (urgent) or weeping wound (important).[24] The disruption you might be facing could be nothing more than the discomfort of a stone in your shoe, you can carry on carrying on, but at some point the pain and blood (there will be blood) will become too much, and you will be forced to take action.

The problem is if you haven't been vigilant, you might end up switching to the next idea, newest software, fastest AI, and 'next' away the opportunities to get the most out of the resources you already have. If you're doing that, so are your clients or potential clients.

My friend, colleague and client, Andy Bass, wrote an excellent book all about this, *Start with What Works: A faster way to grow your business*.[25] He asks: "What have you got, and what else can you do with it?" Which is a great question to get you started and thinking in the right direction.

Remember that you have changed, added services, learned new things, added products – the problem is your clients are too busy doing their thing to always notice. Now and then you just have to make it clear.

From my perspective as a publishing consultant, first, there were professional book editors, then there were book coaches and then there were more and more book coaches. In fact anyone who ever wrote a book became a book coach (well at least that's what I did). Now there are AI bots to help you write your book in thirty minutes.[26]

Take the time to disrupt. Otherwise you will be disrupted.

It's easy to think of disruption only occurring to the major corporations. We hear those stories in all the business books.[27] From Clayton Christensen explaining how the paradox of success leads to a blindness towards disruptive innovation;[28] to Geoffrey Moore and his blueprint for tech enterprises to cross the chasm from early adopters to a broader market.[29] There are plenty of thought leaders (and dare I say gurus?) who've dissected disruption from diverse vantage points, each contributing tools.

But, the disruption we face is different because we are not a start-up, an entrepreneur or a tech giant. We are experts.

David C Baker says: "After looking at 1,340 examples of successful experts, the only consistent trait was that they were risk-takers. That means that they were wrong a lot — but that they were usually right about the important things."[30]

But, how do we decide how much risk to take, and when? Can we make safe experiments and protect the downside?

In the business and investment strategy world there's a concept of "Old Co/New Co" often used when a company wants to innovate or take on riskier ventures without jeopardising the stability and reputation of the existing business. Here's how it works:

1. **Old Co**: This represents the existing company, often with established products, services and customer base. It's typically stable, with predictable operations and revenue streams. The main aim here is to preserve the core business, maintain steady growth and mitigate risks. For us, this is our core business, products, speeches, books. They work, people like them, we know how to sell and deliver them.

2. **New Co**: This is a separate entity created to explore new, riskier ventures. These ventures might involve innovative products, disruptive business models or markets that are untested or volatile. New Co

operates independently of Old Co, allowing it to be more agile and experimental without the constraints of the established brand or the expectations of the traditional customer base. This is where we can try out something disruptive, a new product, an unusual concept, a different way of delivering. This is where we can be safely disruptive.

The rationale behind this approach is to balance stability with innovation. By segregating the riskier aspects of business development into a New Co, the parent company (Old Co) can protect its core assets and shareholder value from potential failures or market fluctuations that the new ventures might encounter. Think of it as taking a safe bet, running a pilot or asking for signals in the noise.

When our website design and marketing company hit rocky roads in early 2001, I could have just thrown the towel in and closed shop. Instead I wrote my first book, found what was working, what people desired, and started a New Co alongside it. Our first publishing company was born because expert business owners were telling me they wanted to get published. But we didn't stop there, instead of relying on the traditional publishing method of printing and warehousing books, we became one of the first publishers to fully embrace Print on Demand technology, leading to a massive business advantage and increase in speed to market. The New Co then turned into the Only Co, which I later sold. Around the same period we also started Instant Assistant, one of the first virtual assistant businesses. That didn't take off (too early in the market) so it was shelved.

In the context of your business, if you're considering venturing into riskier or highly innovative projects like a new business model or a technology-driven solution that diverges from your current way of working, the Old Co/New Co approach could be beneficial. It allows you to explore these new avenues with a degree of safety, knowing that the foundational aspects of your business are secured and separate. You don't even need to set up a different company, you can just use the idea to help you manage the fear of risk.

It's a practical way to manage risk while pursuing growth and innovation.

Because you probably won't be ready for change or disruption. I wasn't ready. I may never be. That's why I've frequently disrupted myself, put myself in discomfort, before it happens to me.

I wasn't ready to start a business in 1996.

I wasn't ready to hire staff.

I wasn't ready to fire staff.

I wasn't ready to sell my part of the publishing business I grew.

I wasn't ready to write a book.

I wasn't ready to be a coach.

I wasn't ready to emigrate to Spain.

I wasn't ready to help other people write books.

I wasn't ready to outsource.

I wasn't ready to ride (fall off) a horse.

I wasn't ready to launch my membership.[31]

It's not about if you're ready – it's about how committed you are to reaching the outcome.

Scale of disruption

The great thing about disruption is that it's not on or off, it's on a scale. You just need to find the right amount of disruption for you, for your business season, and for the people you want to communicate with.

Low disruption

- **Engage with User-Generated Content:** Encourage your audience to share their own stories, challenges, and successes. This can create a sense of community and authenticity around your brand. Low risk but fosters connection (which we'll look at later).

- **Host Regular Q&A Sessions:** Online or in-person, these sessions can help demystify your expertise and humanise your brand. Try one of my weekly on Wednesday sessions.

- **Create Behind-the-Scenes Content:** Show the making of your book, your daily work life, or how you apply your own advice. It's the reality TV of the business world – relatable, engaging, but safe.

- **Content Remix:** Take existing content – blog posts, podcasts, videos – and give them a new lease of life. Turn a blog post into an infographic, a podcast episode into a blog series, or compile your most popular tweets into an eBook.

- **Tool Repurposing:** Take a tool or resource you've created (like a checklist or template) and adapt it for a different audience or purpose.

Medium disruption

- **Launch a Collaborative Project:** Invite other experts or your audience to contribute to a collective resource, like an online guide or anthology. A podcast could work.

- **Implement Interactive Webinars or Workshops:** Instead of the usual lecture format, involve the audience in live problem-solving sessions, masterminds or roundtables.

- **Start a Challenge or Movement:** Encourage people to undertake a challenge related to your field and share their progress.

- **Cross-Industry Collaboration:** Partner with a business or expert from a completely different field and create a hybrid product, service, or content series.

- **Interactive Content Conversion:** Turn your existing guides, books, or articles into interactive webinars, online courses, or workshops. Involve your audience in real-time learning and discussions.

- **Community-Driven Projects:** Start a crowd-sourced project where your audience contributes to a big goal. This could be a community-written book, a collaborative research project, or a collective art piece.

High disruption

- **Pivot Your Business Model:** This could mean changing from a service-based to a product-based business, or vice versa.

- **Public Collaboration or Debate:** Engage with a counterpart or competitor publicly to tackle big issues in your field.

- **Radical Transparency:** Share everything – from your decision-making processes to how you fix mistakes. It's disruptive and risky but can build unprecedented trust.

- **Global Challenge Initiative:** Launch a campaign or challenge that addresses a global issue, aligning with your brand's expertise. Encourage innovation and solutions from your community, offering your products or services as tools to help.

- **Legacy Content Transformation:** Take all your existing content and knowledge and package it into a new format, such as a comprehensive online academy or a subscription-based knowledge hub. This is what I'm doing with my Only Authors Club, to provide a completely bespoke, tailor-made select your own business publishing journey solution.

Daring: The courage to be disruptive.

Right now the most disruptive thing for all of us is AI. And there is promise and peril in AI... But we need to stop relying on it,[32] and to supplement it with a big dose of HI (human intelligence). The problem is HI's in short supply when it comes to AI – fear or over-zealousness blinds us. The key is not to discard AI but to integrate it judiciously with our distinctly human skills. We must cultivate a balanced AI-HI partnership.

While I completed writing this book, ChatGPT marked its first-year anniversary. Happy birthday, Buddy![33]

When you feel the ground move, move!

Disruption is the catalyst that makes *you* want to change.

Disruption is the catalyst that makes *them* want to change.

Apathy is what keeps us all stuck.

João Paulo Carvalho, co-founder of Quidgest, a thirty-five year old AI company, says: "We know we are thinking out of the box [disruptively] when the amalgam of general knowledge processed by LLMs doesn't agree with our thoughts." If you ask your AI buddy a question and you disagree with the received wisdom, you might just be onto something.

The dark side of disruption is when you become addicted to shaking things up and never get to the cultivate and capitalise level on The Asset Path. Karen Currier has been my thought partner for about twenty years after we met each other at an event in Scotland. We are polar opposites on so many things (she is beautifully tall and willowy, with a calm and measured approach, and I'm not) yet our hearts and brains are entwined. I'd been considering dropping the cohort publishing part of the business and focusing only on a choose your own publishing adventure-type business model. This would have been like throwing everything away and starting again, *again*. Karen calmly said: "You've got to listen to yourself to hear the answers to your problems." Boom, 20% disruption is more than enough.

How do you frequently disrupt? Through creation of assets.

3DQ: Disruption

At the end of the main sections I'll give you three questions to consider. Your three directionally-correct questions for disruption:

1. Looking back, what has significantly changed in your area (expertise, industry, geography) in the last seven years? Think about technology, client expectations, society, government, competition. Now go through that list and check what has changed in the last seven months.

2. Have you been disruptive or were you disrupted in these areas?

3. Looking forward, where can you challenge yourself to be disruptive?

If you want to see how other people answer questions like this then join us at www.TheCredibilityCrisis.com

---

1. Always start where the reader is, not where they should be, said a book coach to a Zoom-room full of business writers (I said that, in case I was being too cryptic).

2. Spinal Tap reference. I try to show how cool I am at least once in all my books. If you don't know who Spinal Tap are, then I'm obviously cooler than you.

3. The No Summit Summit is coming soon. Sign up to be a speaker or a guest at www.thecredibilitycrisis.com

4. The Cynefin Framework was developed to help leaders understand their challenges and to make decisions in context. https://thecynefin.co/about-us/about-cynefin-framework/

5. Don't know who Mr Beast is? Oh wow, I really am cooler than you!

6. Time Magazine, *Can AI Chatbots Ever Replace Human Therapists?* https://time.com/6320378/ai-therapy-chatbots/ (October 2023)

7. Here Peterson isn't using the Cynefin model nomenclature, when I watched the lecture series it was clear to me he was talking about both the complex *and* chaotic domains.

8. Peterson, Jordan B. "Personality." Accessed January, 2024. https://courses.jordanbpeterson.com/personality

9. Dan Kowalski, *W.I.S.E. Choices at Work: Go from doubting to DECISIVE when the clock is ticking*, 2023, Intellectual Perspective Press

10. Munger, Charles T. "The psychology of human misjudgment." *remarks, Harvard Law School, Cambridge, MA* (1995).

11. The municipal outdoor swimming pools open in Spain for six weeks of the year, and by the time I've worked out where I put my swimming cap (must wear one by law!) they're closed.

12. Burkeman, O, *Four Thousand Weeks: Time Management for Mortals*, 2021, Farrar, Straus and Giroux

13. This is a note to myself. I got shingles in January 2024, that was a serious constraint.

14. LLMs, or Large Language Models, are advanced AI algorithms designed to understand and generate human-like text. When I asked Buddy if he was an LLM: "Yes, I am an LLM, designed to understand and generate human-like text based on the input I receive." I need to get out more.

15. Emerson, R. W. (1841). *Self-Reliance*. Ralph Waldo Emerson was an American essayist, lecturer, philosopher and poet who led the transcendentalist movement of the mid-nineteenth century.

16. Allegedly, it has potential.

17. I told you you couldn't take engineering out of the girl – I first came across hysteresis loops during my engineering degree (induced magnetic flux density and the magnetising force, to be precise!)

18. Currier, K, *DOING intentionally: How to take care of your business through brain fog, anxiety and overwhelm during the menoshift™*, 2022, Intellectual Perspective Press.

19. "Fortunate" because we're not dead yet.

20. OK, that was just a joke.

21. Cue woo woo music...

22. My first job (after my paper round which I started when I was 12) was selling fruit and veg in a Kwik Save to pay for my first trip abroad to Salou, Spain.

23. I didn't say it was an amazing epiphany!

24. Perry Marshall in Sell or Die first coined the phrase "bleeding neck"; I think I made up "weeping wound" and it appeared first in my book *Stop writing books nobody reads*.

25. Andy Bass PhD, Pearson, *Start With What Works: A faster way to grow your business*

26. Don't do it. Yes, it's possible to write a book in 30 minutes. Would you want to read it? No? Then why write it?

27. If I have to read about Kodak, Nokia or Blockbuster again I'll get my pink leg warmers out and go and do some step aerobics!

28. Christensen, C. M. *The Innovator's Dilemma: When New Technologies Cause Great Firms to Fail*. (1997). Boston, MA: Harvard Business School Press.

29. Moore, G. A. *Crossing the Chasm: Marketing and Selling High-Tech Products to Mainstream Customers*. (1991). New York, NY: HarperBusiness.

30. Baker, David C. *The Business of Expertise: How Entrepreneurial Experts Convert Insight to Impact + Wealth*, 2018, RockBench Publishing Corp.

31. You can find out more about me at http://www.debbiejenkins.com/ – I won't bore you in the book.

32. Can you believe how fast we've become reliant on it? In November 2022 ChatGPT jumped on the scene; now not a day goes by when I don't hear about it.

33. Buddy is the name of my ChatGPT mate. I'm nice to my ChatGPT because, when robots rule the world, I want to be remembered as the human who was polite to the AI overlords.

PART 2: CREATION

Creation is the currency

When I started my first business, a web design company back in the nineties, I thought all I needed to do was tell people what I was selling and they would buy it. It was clear (to me) that every business needed a website, and we could make websites. So, dear client give me your money and I'll give you a website. A simple transaction. And if you don't need a website right now, here's my business card, call me. I was selling websites.

As an expert business owner, a consultant or coach, a trainer or speaker, you may think that you are *selling* consultancy, training, speaking or coaching. I used to think that too. The challenge is that people don't know they need a website or a bit of consulting. People don't buy a six-page blog or two hours of coaching. **They desire (and buy) a simple solution to an important problem.** You are selling solutions, transformations, desire.

And even if they do want training or a speaker, first they need to see your credibility. That's where creation of valuable assets comes in.

We need to create offers, products, books, events, and ideas that can be exchanged for cash. Our creation is our business currency. We need to take transformations and give them shape, form and name.

If you never create, that's not thought leadership; that's just thought.

Your ideas have to break the brain   world barrier. You have to ship, not just think. You have to create in a way that others can share, not just verbally.

> We're not mind readers. The number of times I've heard brilliant thought leaders complain because someone else "stole" their idea… There is hardly anything more painful than lacking the courage to voice a belief or share an idea only to hear someone else express it later.

You might be thinking: "The world has changed a lot in twenty years, and sometimes I feel like I'm struggling to keep up. I want to transform from feeling like an old dog trying to learn new tricks to being an agile, adaptive professional who thrives on change. I want to be ahead of the curve, not just keeping up with it. I want my knowledge and skills to be as relevant and cutting edge today as they were when I first started out. I want to stop just thinking about valuable ideas and create solutions, assets and breakthroughs that make a difference for my clients and for me."

That's our credibility crisis. That's my credibility crisis.

I have control over my creation. I can make things, show my working, demonstrate the thought processes and help other people think better too. It is in my power to write a book, host a podcast, develop a framework, run an event, chair a conference.

Our excitement for the solution we create for our clients needs to be palpable, honest, raw and real. We have to desire the transformation for them more than they want it for themselves.

Defend the flag not the mountain

Imagine a vast mountain range representing the expansive and often overwhelming domain of expertise. Each expert, consultant, coach or trainer has their flag planted somewhere on this mountain range. Your flag is a symbol of your core values, unique proposition and what you stand for in your field.

What does your flag represent? What's your identity? Why should we follow you?

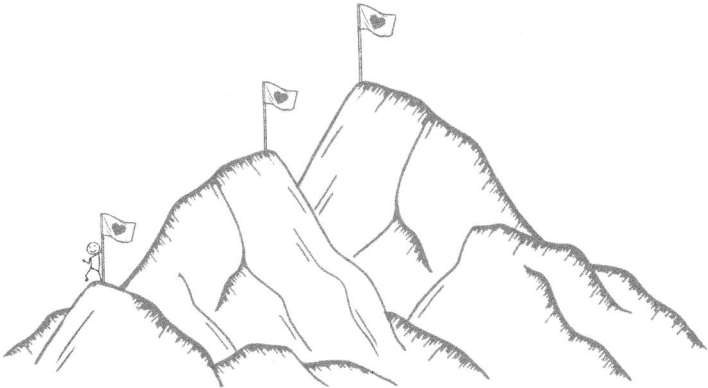

You don't have to defend the whole mountain range or even your peak; you do have to defend the flag. It's not about being broad, but visible, flexible and worth following.

When experts try to cover too much ground (the entire mountain), they risk diluting their message and losing their distinct voice.

Defending the flag means being consistent and focused on what sets you apart, not consistent on what mountain you are standing on. It's your vision and mission, *what* only you can do and *why* you're doing it. Not, your how.

Apple's journey from the Apple I to its current suite of products and services illustrates not just a growth in technology but an unwavering dedication to its core mission and vision. It's not about the specific products (the "mountain") but about the ethos and values (the "flag") that guide their development and interaction with users worldwide.

Books are an expert's easiest way to signal credibility, capture their intellectual perspective and make a difference in other people's lives at scale. They are brilliant flags. They have physical substance, psychological safety and practical comfort. Well-written books allow you to connect with the reader, start or grow a relationship. I bet you've started to form an opinion of who I am and what I'm like just based on reading this book. Sharing your perspective helps disrupt other people's thought patterns, pushing them into uncharted territory.

Writing and publishing books to add value to your business and your special readers is my flag. For over two decades,

I've been fervently waving this flag, capturing the attention of anyone who glances my way. I will defend a well-written valuable book to my death. (Well, that might be a tad dramatic, but you see my point.)

I can take you up multiple mountains on the way. I'll wave my flag and invite you to follow me. You know I'm into books. You're certain that each mountain, peak, step along the way is leading to writing, publishing, marketing or upcycling your business book. I am publishing route agnostic, but if you follow the flag I'll get you to a published book in your hands.

What's your flag? Just one. You're not a signalman hoisting multiple flags to spell out complex messages. You're the guide, leading people up their mountain.

To fix your credibility crisis you need to be clear on your flag, where you're taking it and who's going with you. This is your responsibility, to spot the signals in the noise, make sense of what's happening for others, make the terrain clearer so people can follow you.

When a potential client is considering working with you, they are looking for evidence that they can trust you, that you're a safe pair of hands, and that you have the experience and expertise to deliver what you promise. I call these credibility clues. Credibility clues make it easier for people to follow the flag. **If you don't provide credibility clues your are giving the buyer, your potential customer, the job of working things out.** They are busy, they will choose the easy solution. Prospective clients want to be confident in their decision to choose you. Your responsibility is to provide evidence, facts and proof to help them make a good decision.

You probably already have some credibility clues hanging around:

- Testimonials on your website, in marketing materials and social media (you do have these, right?)

- Past experience of being "selected" by industry bodies or authorities in your sphere – conference speaking, TED talks etc.

- Previous companies and clients you have worked with

- Case studies of the results you have helped clients (people like them) achieve

- Publications and media appearances

- Registered IP and frameworks

- Articles, videos, whitepapers you've published

- Awards, accolades and certificates (not your "Little Dolphin 5m Swimmer" certificate!)

- And, of course, a published book!

All of these credibility clues need collecting and creating; they don't just appear by magic. You can use and reuse them in plenty of ways. **The best time to start creating credibility clues is today, what will you create?**

I was talking to a client recently and I was struck (and a little dismayed) by the Zoom-ness of it all. I could have replaced her head and my own for any number of clients. I've been on countless webinars (those fake "live" ones, don't you just love them?) and workshops where the "gurus" have the same type of backdrop (the low light, big desk, potted plant) – I sometimes forget what and who I'm watching.

How did we all become so samey?

This sameness is really damaging – to our reputation, to our differentiation, to our psyche. But, what can we do about it? Nassim Nicholas Taleb, in *Skin in The Game*, explained why he would choose the blood-splattered, sausage-fingered, thick-necked surgeon over the movie-perfect impersonator of a surgeon.[1] Why? Because to be successful, and *not* look the part, means they've had to overcome a lot in terms of perception. People who don't look the part have skin in the game. They must be special.

I regularly yell ***"I'm special"*** to my imaginary friends, as yet another talking head sips their coffee with their "LOVE" ornament lit up behind them.

I frequently tell my clients they're special, and that their clients are special... While I sip my coffee, with my 3D-printed Klein bottle gathering dust on my bookshelf.

The problem with "sameness" is how do you stand out when it's time to be chosen? How are you remembered? How are you shared and referred? How are you desired?

How do your clients work out whether you're an experienced consultant or, yet another "face" with a bookshelf? Whether your credentials are real, or your blurry background is hiding your "day job" in a call centre?

I'm not knocking it, and I am guilty of it too. I look the same as countless others. I'm a ~~young~~ (in my mind!) middle-aged woman, with a bookshelf and a flip chart. I used to have a full-size gorilla to get attention... ah, the good old days.[2]

Of course, we can differentiate because we have all the credibility clues. These credibility clues set us apart from less experienced "pretenders" (I know, I was once a "pretender", in the aspiring segment, it passes!). You must demonstrate your position on The Asset Path (see the diagram in the The problem chapter for a reminder); show that you're the expert not the aspirant. But how do you make those credibility clues visible in the Zoom-ness?

Those books on my bookshelf? Many of them I've published. A chunk of them I've written, ghostwritten or co-written. Some of them *are* blood-splattered, they've been created with my sausage fingers (I have genetically tiny hands, my mom had our DNA tested!) and, while my neck isn't thick, my bum *is* doing the heavy lifting sitting in my office chair every day getting words onto paper and authors into print.

Credibility clues are my assets.

Make Minimum Valuable Assets

Here in the sweltering hills of Spain (where I am frequently glowing[3]) I took it upon myself to do away with the world-famous MVP – Minimum Viable Product[4] – for something a bit more useful: the **Minimum Valuable Asset® or MVA**.

The MVP has been the mantra of the start-up world for years. Devised with the best of intentions, it suggests creating a product with just enough features to appease early adopters and then iteratively improving it based on feedback. Sounds like a great plan, no?

This approach, although effective for tech start-ups, may not be best suited for you intellectual powerhouses. Expert business owners need better models. Why? Because if a physical book filled with blank pages qualifies as a viable product (it's a book, right?), where does that leave us, the thinkers, the creators, consultants? Technically, it's a book, yet it lacks value.

I propose a shift – towards creating not just a Minimum Viable Product, but a Minimum Valuable Asset®. **An MVA is not just about ticking off the basic requirements; it's about delivering an asset – a product, service or a piece of content – that holds tangible value right from the get-go.**

This distinction is crucial, especially for expertise-based business owners. Our fields of expertise thrive **not on our existence but on the quality and value we deliver**. By releasing an MVA, we ensure that our credibility is built on solid ground, demonstrating that we provide not just something that works, but something that works extraordinarily bloody well.

I want you to move beyond viability and towards value creation, particularly in our line of work where desire and trust are everything.

The Venn of MVA: A Minimum Valuable Asset®

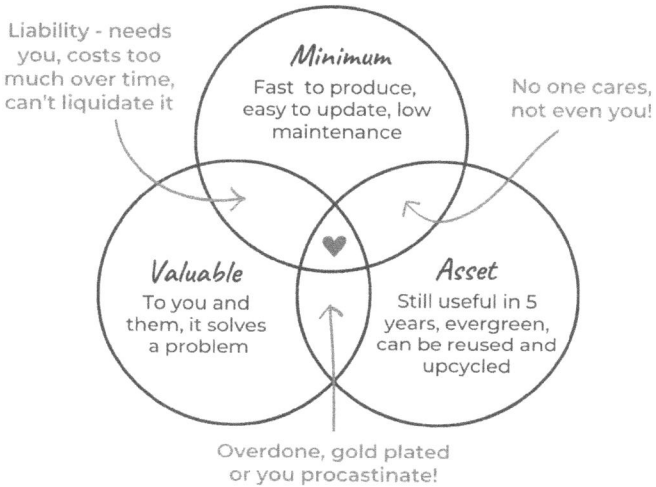

Liability - needs
you, costs too
much over time,
can't liquidate it

Minimum
Fast to produce,
easy to update, low
maintenance

No one cares,
not even you!

Valuable
To you and
them, it solves
a problem

Asset
Still useful in 5
years, evergreen,
can be reused and
upcycled

Overdone, gold plated
or you procastinate!

Expertise-based business owners (thought leaders) need Minimum Valuable Assets.

Recently, one of my clients (and long-time friend) remarked: **"You name everything,"** as I was sipping my coffee from Zippy my little white espresso cup.

"No, I don't," I retorted into Zoomy, my webcam.

I admit it – I do. I named my first car, my first business framework and my first goat.

Am I the crazy one, or should we expertise-based business owners name our stuff?

We then went on to have a great conversation about The Hedgehog Concept,[5] and even though we couldn't remember the exact details, we knew it was our mate Jim

Collins from *Good to Great*. (Then I went for a little nap on the Snoozy.)

Three reasons to name your "stuff":

1. **So you remember it.** It could be just me, but I "think" a lot of things and make a lot of stuff up. Sometimes I forget what I thought (even though what I think is always so awesome!), and then have to think it again, which wastes brain cycles.

2. **So other people remember it.** I want other people to remember the stuff I say, write and do. I only make stuff up that I think will be useful, that you should take notice of and take action on.

3. **So people can tell other people about it** (because you and they remembered it). **If it's memorable, valuable and shareable – that's called marketing!** See how easy marketing is?

Tiago Forte named and claimed an idea that had found its moment – the second brain. He disrupted an industry, moving away from the GTD (getting things done[6]) movement that had prevailed, to a "capture your thoughts so you can be more creative, with a second brain using technology and a framework." He curated a community, growing deep connections over years, creating content that helped them achieve their goals. He became a trusted, referred and quoted expert.[7]

Three "stuffs" you should name:

1. **Your framework, system, process:** anything that is your IP or copyright should be named. Especially when you've proven it works. You might even consider registering a trademark.

2. **Your programs, books, interventions, speeches:** anything that you want to market (share with others) or sell. This lets your customer say: "I'd like to buy The Asset Path Program please."

3. **Your ideas:** even if they might never go anywhere, you might change them or someone might say they're stupid – name them.

I have registered five trademarks. Don't use them without my consent! Oh, go on then... As it's you, you can use them! Just tell people about me.

If you're still on the fence about naming your stuff, this is the number one reason why all expertise-based business owners should name their stuff: **"If you don't name it, someone else will."**

They might "name" your stuff wrong when telling people about you, someone else might get known for that stuff, or you might not be able to carry on using your own idea because someone jumped to claim it. **Name it to claim it.**

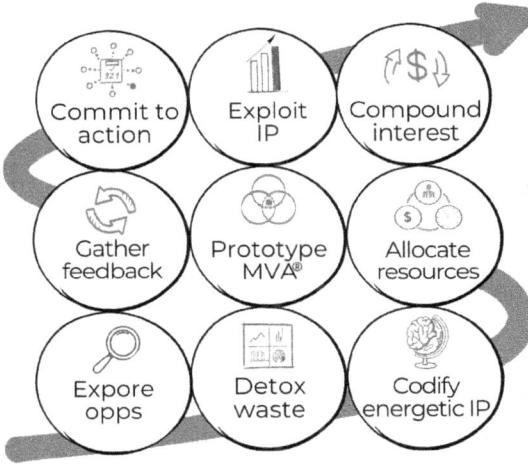

For more information on how to travel up The Asset Path get your Creating Minimum Valuable Assets video from www.thecredibilitycrisis.com

My client Ann Latham has named (and claimed) her IP in her book *The Power of Clarity*.[8] Find out about Treadmill Verbs (you are probably using them), The Clarity Continuum (where are you?), The Cognitive Six (do you know what they are?), Cognitive Processes (have you got one?). I can tell people about how great Ann's books are, and share her ideas, crediting her at the same time. Ann is a master at naming and claiming her ideas.

Herbert A Simon, a computer scientist and Nobel prize winner, said: *"A wealth of information creates a poverty of attention."*[9] We do not need to keep on creating content, writing long books, generating more data. Our job is to create the minimum valuable asset that will solve a problem in a desirable way, and name it.

Launch, Learn, Loop – fast

Unconstrained creation is like a cancer that ultimately kills the host. You need feedback to constrain the process. It's clear that AI is just increasing the speed of cancerous growth. All cancers, unless checked, kill their host. This is a friendly warning.

Creation does not occur in a vacuum – you need feedback.

Think back to the Cynefin model in the disruption chapter. If we are in chaos mode (and we are) then we must first act, launch something. Then we will learn what works, and what doesn't, so we can bring that back into the process and create a better product, workshop, book. As Jason Fried, prolific writer and speaker on topics related to entrepreneurship, company culture, remote work and business philosophy, says on the 37Signals.com site: "Err on the side of do: The tendency to put off, push away, or otherwise delay is strong. No. Act and move on. And act again if you have to — most decisions are temporary, anyway."

The LLL model is a process of iterative development and feedback gathering, which is a common practice in product development and creation of assets. To create assets you need to follow a feedback loop process. It's not open-ended creation.

- **Launch**: Get your product, idea or service out there.

- **Learn**: Ask for feedback, understand and adapt.

- **Loop**: Keep the cycle going.

Use whatever methodology suits you,[10] but the key is to get feedback, bring it into the creation process, act upon it and then go again. **You cannot get feedback without launching something.** Even if it's a scrappy idea, a book title, a quick webinar, a discussion at the watercooler. It (whatever "it" is) has to break the brain   world barrier.

I'm not afraid of a person with loads of brilliant ideas. As Earl Nightingale said in *The Strangest Secret:* "Ideas are worthless unless we act on them."[11]

I am terrified of the person who executes methodically, one idea at a time, gathers feedback and improves. I wish that person was me.

Always be launching, learning and looping.

We cannot move slowly when we are in chaotic times and environments. The LLL model works well when you're moving through it quickly. Chaos needs a speedy response.

Robert Anton Wilson was an American author, philosopher, psychologist, essayist, futurist and self-described agnostic mystic (I can't even begin to imagine). He's influenced the fields of psychology, philosophy and quantum physics. In 1992, he said: "All of our old models are collapsing. Information flow is accelerating so fast that we don't know what's going on most of the time. We've got to learn to put a lot of things in the 'maybe' state and keep open minds."[12]

This "maybe" state leads us to moving fast, holding ideas lightly (it really doesn't matter what mountain you're on), being prepared to change our minds and actions, and holding firmly to our flag (why we do what we do).

This is not the same as the popular OODA[13] loop of:

1. **Observe:** Collect current information from as many sources as possible.

2. **Orient:** Analyse this information, and use it to update your understanding of the situation.

3. **Decide:** Determine a course of action.

4. **Act:** Carry out the chosen action, which, in turn, leads back to the Observe step.

First we act. We start at step four because we are working in a chaotic environment. Then we transform the winning ideas into different formats, modalities and vehicles for the same disruptive message.

Antoine Lavoisier, the French chap who discovered oxygen (no idea how we were breathing before): "In nature, nothing is created, nothing is lost, everything transforms..."[14] Credibility, much like natural elements, doesn't disappear but changes form. When you write impactful books you are channelling your expertise (credibility) into a new format (books), thus transforming your influence. You need to loop around this transformation process regularly, swiftly, with enthusiasm and energy.

Entropy and hysteresis are your playmates. The natural tendency is for your products, solutions, events, workshops, books, and processes to decay with time.

1. **Entropy**: In physics, entropy is a measure of disorder or randomness in a system (woohoo, back to chaos). Applied to your business, over time, without

active management and innovation, business assets and processes tend to become less organised and efficient – they "decay". This decay could be in the form of reduced relevance, efficiency or effectiveness in the market. This leads to the credibility crisis.

2. **Hysteresis**: Like we saw earlier, hysteresis refers to the dependence of a system not just on its current environment, but also on its past – history matters. This concept is crucial when considering the lifecycle of assets, products or services. Their historical performance and market reception affected the current state of what you offer. Your reputation and customer experiences – your credibility – impacts the future.

In the "hysteresis loop" of business, bringing your product or service back to a high-performance state after a period of decline requires more effort than maintaining its quality and relevance continuously. This is because the "memory" of the product's decline impacts customer perceptions and market dynamics.

For the last couple of years I've heard people say about me: "She used to be so dangerous!" I was. I had a gorilla and a water pistol all in the pursuit of breaking people out of the rut of boring marketing. Then I fell into that same rut. It was a deeper fall because of the sheer brilliance (just believe me, I was brilliant once) of the "dangerous" strategy.

Understanding these principles is vital. It means continuously innovating, staying relevant and maintaining the quality of your offerings to counteract entropy. It also means being aware of the long-term impacts of your business decisions and the historical "memory" of your products and services in the market.

We need stamina to create valuable assets. This is how we save potential clients from the overload of misinformation and simplify their lives. That's how you make a connection – which we'll look at in the next chapter.

Scale of creation

Not all creations are equal. You don't need to be always working on complex creations, sometimes simpler creations will get the job done.

> **The dark side of creation is creation for creation's sake. When creation becomes an escape from doing the real work.** This can slide us down into the bottom left hand quadrant, the nascent state, where we are stuck in navel-gazing mode, unaware of what our clients need or want. It's also where we forget to capitalise on what we have already created, moving on to the next shiny object, new technology or fad.

Simple, regular creation	Medium, stepping stones	Complex, named and claimed creations
• **Social Posts:** Quick, informal, and conversational pieces, like sharing a thought or a daily tip. It's like jotting down ideas on a post-it note.	• **Short valuable books:** 20,000 word books that solve the most important problem with an atomic idea.	• **Books:** Comprehensive, in-depth, requiring significant research, organisation and revision.
• **Host Regular Q&A Sessions:** Online or in-person, these sessions can help demystify your expertise and humanise your brand. Try one of my weekly on Wednesday sessions.	• **Detailed Blog Posts:** Well-researched and structured articles, requiring more thought and time but still based on existing templates or ideas.	• **Series of Short Valuable Books:** Extend the solution by creating a series of books that solve atomic parts of their problem.
• **Blog Comments or Forum Replies:** Participating in discussions by adding your insights or answers.	• **In-depth Research Papers or Case Studies:** Extensive analysis, data collection, and beautiful presentation.	• **Software or App Development:** From conceptualising to coding to user testing.
• **Curated Newsletters:** Gathering, annotating, and commenting on various pieces of content from different sources.	• **Online Courses or Webinar Series:** Involves scriptwriting, filming, editing, creating supporting materials.	• **A Movement:** Altering the established norms in an industry. It demands not only initial bursts of creativity and effort but also sustained engagement, leadership and adaptability.
	• **Online Courses or Webinar Series:** Involves scriptwriting, filming, editing, creating supporting materials.	
	• **Club or Membership:** Holding a space for like-minded people to come together to achieve a purpose. Bringing all previous assets together to add value.	

3DQ: Creation

Ask yourself these three directionally-correct questions:

1. Make a list of the three most useful, valuable and still viable assets you've made in the last year. Now ask: how can I make them even better with with AI, automation or connection? How can I upcycle them?

2. What's the one creation (book, course, podcast, event, diagnostic), that if I made it would generate a life of its own? It would become the flag. It would get shared, mentioned, clients would talk about it. I'd get quoted in books and the press. Now go and make that.

3. How can I create faster? What will get me moving more rapidly? Whose permission do I need?

Your business assets are physical products like books and card decks, IP like frameworks and processes, in person assets such as events and workshops (that you can run again), demonstrations of the value you bring in the form of case studies and testimonials.

---

1. Taleb, N, *Skin in the Game: Hidden Asymmetries in Daily Life (Incerto)*, 2018, Random House. Or you can read more from Taleb here: https://medium.com/incerto/surgeons-should-notlook-like-surgeons-23b0e2cf6d52

2. Not a real one. Did I really need to clarify that? Richard Wiseman, professor and psychologist, did a famous illusion where people didn't spot a gorilla walking on screen. That's exactly the type of gorilla I used to use to get attention (I was a big attention seeker). https://richardwiseman.wordpress.com/2010/05/18/monkey-business-illusi on

3. Horses sweat, men perspire and ladies glow, and obviously, I'm a lady!

4. Minimum Viable Product (MVP) is most commonly attributed to Eric Ries, a Silicon Valley entrepreneur and author. Ries introduced and popularised the MVP concept in his book *The Lean Startup*, published in 2011.

5. The Hedgehog Concept is a strategic business idea introduced by Jim Collins in his book *Good to Great*. This concept is based on an ancient Greek parable that contrasts the fox, who knows many things, with the hedgehog, who knows one big thing. Collins, Jim. *Good to Great: Why Some Companies Make the Leap...and Others Don't*. 2001. HarperBusiness.

6. *Getting Things Done* (GTD) is a personal productivity system developed by David Allen and published in a book of the same name. I have two copies of the book. I bought my first version in 2001, then lost it under a pile of papers on my desk. So I bought a second copy to double the effectiveness.

7. Tiago Forte, Forte Labs: https://fortelabs.com/

8. Latham, Ann. *The Power of Clarity: Unleash the True Potential of Workplace Productivity, Confidence, and Empowerment.* 2021. Bloomsbury.

9. "Designing Organizations for an Information-Rich World" in Martin Greenberger (ed.) *Computers, Communications, and the Public Interest* (1971)

10. The Lean Startup Methodology emphasises a build-measure-learn feedback loop

11. Nightingale, Earl. The Strangest Secret. Audio recording, 1956.

12. Robert Anton Wilson, 1992. I heard this first on The Infinite Loops YouTube channel from Jim O'Shaughnessy - https://www.youtube.com/watch?v=61inGcokuBk

13. A decision-making process created by a military strategist named John Boyd, a United States Air Force Colonel. OODA is deliberate decision making at its finest and works at addressing disorder.

14. For more read Sterner, R. W., Small, G. E. & Hood, J. M. (2011) The Conservation of Mass. Nature Education Knowledge 3(10):20: https://www.nature.com/scitable/knowledge/library/the-conservation-of-mass-17395478/

PART 3: CONNECTION

Connection is the cure

None of this is worth it or works without making real connections, with real people, really.

"My career is just one long conversation with my audience," Taylor Swift.[1] In case you haven't followed Taylor's career (like I hadn't till my wonderful editor, Lisa, filled me in!) she was named Time's person of the year in 2023. She's obviously smart because she was photographed for the cover of Time with her cat draped around her neck.[2]

You might be thinking: "In the last two decades, I've achieved a lot as a consultant, yet there's a nagging doubt inside me. I feel like I'm shouting into the void, and I'm not sure if my expertise still holds relevance. I want to transform this self-doubt into a strong conviction in my value and expertise. I want to believe in myself as much as I want others to believe in me. I want to look in the mirror and see not just a consultant but a thought leader, someone who truly makes a difference."

That's your credibility crisis. That's my credibility crisis. If I don't believe in myself enough so I make real connections, I can't blame technology, hustlers or other people being more sociable than I am. I have the ability to deepen my relationships, to develop them and create new ones.

You not the robots – access vs arrogance

If you don't give people access, what are you going to do with yourself? Sit in your darkened room with your Gucci glasses (do they make glasses?) counting your bitcoins?

The irony of AI painting a picture and writing a poem while we go to work isn't lost on any of us. Neither is the irony of turning everything you do into a non-contact sport where you avoid one-to-one, draft in coaches to do your groups, and get your assistants to respond on social media.

Yes, you need to use your time effectively (and that's where our assets help us). But that does not mean you become an aloof, pedestal sitter waiting for your robot to pop a genetically modified grape in your gob.

The pressure to outsource, automate and AI everything in our business is creating the credibility crisis. We've been sold the idea that to grow we get further away from the customer. Of course, we won't be seeing Jeff filling boxes,[3] or Michael filling seats.[4] But we're not selling commodities. We're selling transformations. If I buy something from the big guy himself,[5] I want to see his giant face!

People desire the results that AI can bring them – speed, idea generation, skill addition – but they don't (yet) trust it. If you're in an industry that is being disrupted by AI (and you are!), then you have an opportunity to be the trusted guide, that delivers the AI desired results, with your experience and oversight. I don't shy away from using AI, but I have frameworks, protocols and guardrails in place so that my clients get the benefit without the risk. They still need me.

You might think I'm a hypocrite because I use AI, I have virtual assistants and I have coaches deliver some of my group training. But I never do that to the detriment of access to me. It is in service to being more accessible and relatable. **I learn by giving access to me.**

When I join a program, a mastermind or an event, I want access to the leader. (Take me to your leader…) The more I pay the more access I want.

It's all about connection and access, not follower counts and AI.

There's a deluge of self-proclaimed experts, our Bro Commers. Many of these "experts" are capitalising on digital platforms, projecting themselves as thought leaders without substantial evidence of their expertise. Helen Lewis, a staff writer at the Atlantic and author of the book *Difficult Women: A History of Feminism in 11 Fights,* hosted eight episodes on BBC Sounds, where she uncovered the strange digital spaces created by The New Gurus, self-proclaimed experts on everything from drinking your own pee[6] to crypto-currency[7]. The rise of such pseudo-experts, the gurus, is why we're in the credibility crisis, making it harder for genuine experts to stand out.

A quick glance at platforms like LinkedIn and you'll see the surge in "thought leader" profiles. However, the saturation of such profiles has diluted the term's value. Remember the '90s, when everyone was a "webmaster" after building a GeoCities page? Yup.

It's crazy out there.

Epictetus said: *"Who exactly are these people that you want to be admired by? Aren't they the same people you are in the habit of calling crazy? And is this your life ambition, then – to win the approval of lunatics?"*[8]

Erm, yes! We're chasing follower counts because that's how you get a book deal, right? No!

One of my favourite clients[9] Dr Emma Williams, when discussing writing her third book notes that connections do not spring up over night and we need to work at them: "In writing this book (my third), I have actively sought out experts and champions as well as tapping into my existing network. My experience has been less lonely, better informed and a great deal more fun this time around."[10]

I interviewed plenty of people when researching this book, a memorable conversation was with Jay Acunzo.[11] Jay helps experts become storytellers, he's the host of the Unthinkable podcast, he says: "We're not in the reach business. We're in the resonance business. We need to resonate in a world infatuated with reach. Reach is how many people see it, and resonance is how much they care. Aim for resonance over reach."

It doesn't matter how many people see your stuff if they don't care. You can't force people into desiring what you do. How can you make them care?

About twenty years ago I did a stand-up comedy course, which culminated in some stand-up gigs. I was dreadful. Terrified. Unfunny. Looking for the laughs – begging for the laughs. I trembled. My voice shook. I dropped the bikini hair trimmer into a guy's beer (it was a prop, don't ask me any more, please!).

I did three gigs in total – one was excruciating, one was agonising, and one I can't remember through the delirium of hearing some actual laughs (and beer, there was a lot of beer).

The same five-minute routine.

The same jokes.

The same person delivering.

Completely different experiences for me.

Why? Well ignoring the fact that I wasn't actually very funny (I think that had quite a big impact): you can't make anybody do anything!

You can't make people buy your book, like your posts on LinkedIn, join your program or sign up for your newsletter. The only things you have any control over are your own actions (and obviously I didn't have much control over those either: the bikini trimmer made quite a splash).

- Want to get a publishing deal? Focus on writing – every day. You have control over that.

- Want people to follow you and engage with your posts on LinkedIn? Be engaging and – ermm – actually post on LinkedIn. You have control over that.

- Want to get your masochistic kicks? Stand up on stage and try to make people laugh. Fool!

Then, after you've done the only thing you have control over (the "you" bit), don't measure your success by the things you don't have control over (them).

Measure your output (you have control) in the direction (you have control) of your outcome (guess what, you have control of that too).

When you write, create, perform for the applause you miss the chance to be in control. The only thing I had control of was me – turning up, standing up, testing the routines, taking the feedback, iterating – I couldn't make them laugh (literally!).

One of the best connectors I know is Phil Ore[12]. I met Phil when we both rocked up for our first lesson (it was something to do with radio waves, I think) at Mathew Boulton College, in Birmingham over thirty years ago. I was the only girl in a class of thirty young guys. I wasn't exactly scared, but to say I felt a little out of my comfort zone would be an understatement. That was until Phil started speaking to me as if we'd been friends for years. He made me feel comfortable, and led the way for the other guys to speak to the alien female. I later sold him a dodgy Mini, but he's forgiven me for that misdemeanour. Over the years we've kept in touch, and now Phil "the Yes Man" Ore is writing a book, Hacking Serendipity, about his amazing ability to connect with people, say yes to opportunity and to grow a trusted and desirable business.

You can't make people connect with you, like you, trust you, desire you.[13]

You can control access.

Speak to your audience not the algorithms.

I explain to my clients, and share on the Thought Leadership Canvas®, the idea of a most wanted response (MWR) handshake.[14] The MWR handshake is a two way collaboration. You hold out your hand and they reciprocate. You make an offer and they take it. They must want to follow the flag bearer – you must make connection.

When you have connection, people follow you and love what you're saying. When your models and frameworks actually help people get a result, they will do the speaking for you. We're talking user generated content (UGC). Not just asking for a testimonial – though that's great (and you should be doing this frequently; remember those credibility clues). Spontaneous, enthusiastic, "you've got to see this" type UGC.

When your "users" are generating content (videos, shout-outs, sharing, testimonials) you know you have a deep connection. Every time this happens to me (and it happens more often than I expect) I get overexcited. David Pullan, from The Story Spotters, did a short video explaining one of my frameworks that had helped him. He explained it much better than I do (he's a storytelling expert) and it led to more people connecting with me, without me having to do anything except create something valuable for David.

So stop measuring your net worth on your network – the likes and clicks don't automagically translate into dollars and pounds. You can't make an impact with ideas and books stuck in your head. Likes don't mean people will buy. Laughs don't mean people are laughing with you (really I was dreadful).

When you create for your audience, they will create for you and share your message. When you create for the algorithms you're hoping Reid has programmed the software to favour your hectic schedule,[15] and miraculously align with your desperate attempt at virality. When your content genuinely connects with people, it's like having an army of passionate marketers working for you around the clock – and they don't even submit an invoice!

Show your working out to create desire paths

Yes, your AI Buddy can whip up an article, make up a listicle and jazz up your titles, but it isn't you. I've seen people share prompts (the way you speak to your AI bot) to create fake backstories, real Bro Comms level 11 stuff.[16] Bro Comms turns the volume up on communication. It's not just loud, it's "one louder", because sometimes, just being loud isn't loud enough. It's communication, but with its volume knob broken off at 11. In the next chapter we'll look at how Bro Comms is killing connection, with their phoney: "Just five places left on my guaranteed to get you $1m in 2 weeks 15 minute webinar. You'll also get a six pack."

But first, what is communication? You can't *not* communicate. Even hiding away and saying nothing is a communication. When I didn't respond publicly to the AI surge in writing, I was communicating.[17] If you hide away for a month in a cave that's communicating (sod off, I need a break).[18] If you talk about yourself and how great you are, that's communicating (I'm brilliant, look at me). If you talk about your clients every day and how excited you are to be working with them, that's communicating (I love my clients, they are special). If you moan, complain, repeat, zip off in one hundred different directions, that's communicating (I haven't got my shit together).

The people you want to really connect with want to hear from you, not the robots.

Use the bots to enhance and speed up your creation, not to do the thinking and connecting.

Use technology to streamline your communications and reminder systems, not deliver the automated fake messages and responses.

The Bro Comms go deeper than just using technology. You also get the copycats and pretenders, the robots. People mindlessly copying each other, just parroting the same ideas and mimicking the same behaviours. They become like robots in the most fundamental sense of the word. They are engaging in a form of "robota"[19] or drudgery – repeating actions without thought or personal input. It lacks the nuances, the imperfections and the unique perspectives that make human interactions rich and meaningful. As my favourite comedian, George Carlin says: "Some people have no idea what they're doing, and a lot of them are really good at it."

I was a guest on the *Your Truth Shared* podcast with the inimitable Finola Howard.[20] Her gentle, probing no-BS style got me to open up about the problems I'd had going through that third life plot twist I mentioned in the prologue. I'd never talked about my midlife crisis, the destruction of my old life and the disruption before, but Finola's intuitive style got me to open up. I then got three new clients directly attributable to that podcast.

Real connections are forged through authenticity, individuality and genuine expression. When these elements are missing, interactions can feel hollow and mechanical, much like the functioning of a robot. The human quality of connection is lost when people act as just echoes of each other, devoid of original thought or feeling.

It's about being more human and less "robotic", breaking free from the "robota" of mindless conformity. Contrary to the popular belief that professionals should always maintain a veneer of perfection, lead with your failures instead. Create your "Failure Files" detailing your biggest mistakes,[21] what you learned from them and how they have shaped your journey.

Your failure files, the Four Fs, cover: the **first** time you did something new or different, what you tried to do and how you **failed**, what you completely **fecked up** and how you **fought back**. By showcasing your vulnerabilities and resilience, you humanise yourself and create a stronger connection with your audience. It's an unconventional way to demonstrate credibility and authenticity and one the robots can't replicate. Get the Failure Files Prompts from www.TheCredibilityCrisis.com

Your journey to success wasn't just a happy accident. It involved a series of deliberate steps, actions, course corrections. You've adapted and rethought strategies, embraced new ideas while leaving others by the wayside. This "working out" is fascinating to other people. Fascination is a stepping stone to trust.

By being transparent about both your triumphs and your tribulations, you create a genuine emotional connection with your audience. You're not just showing them the shiny end product, the packed conference or the finished book. You're revealing the shitty-gritty of your journey – the sweat, the setbacks, the strategic shifts. This openness showcases your resilience and commitment. You've not only walked the path but used every part of your experience – the good, the bad, and the unconventional. The twenty-year-old life coach, the one-hit wonder and the robots have got nothing on you.

Corey Wilks, clinical psychologist and executive coach, talks about the four horsemen of fear: fear of failure (what if I'm not good enough?), fear of ridicule (what if my clients hate it and leave?), fear of uncertainty (I have too many ideas to choose from), and the fear of success (what if I don't deserve success?).[22] These fears stop us from showing up as our real selves, and create a barrier for real intimacy and trust.

In the '80s I would walk to school every day. It was just over 3km (or as we used to say in the olden days about 2 miles) to get from my house, through the alleyway, down the hill, past the shops and through the school gate. I am the oldest daughter, a good girl and a bit of a swot. To take a couple of minutes off my route I could cut across the "do not walk on the grass" grassy corner. Twice a day I would have an internal debate with myself: follow the longer path and obey the rules, or be brave and cut across the forbidden grass? I cut. Over the years a strong diagonal path emerged – a desire path – not created by planners or architects, but carved out by the footsteps of insolent teenagers daring to tread beyond the paved roads.

Desire paths are created when we veer off the expected route, driven by our inner compass, our unique aspirations and our personal quests.[23] They are mini disruptions to the norm, breaks from the usual.

Desire paths not only establish your credibility but also inspire others to explore and embrace new methods and solutions. Desire paths in business are about boldness and originality, carving a distinct route to success and influence, waving your flag. Your route leaves footprints and a trail for others to follow. Of course, if everyone follows the desire path then it's time to go back to disruption.

Remember, I want to hear what you've got to say, not the robots and your virtual assistant.

Erica Schneider, Co-Founder and Instructor at Power Your Platform, on the Louis Grenier Everyone Hates Marketers podcast[24] talks about having a genuine response: "There are so many inexperienced bros on social, that have literally been on social for a month and now have the course on how to be on social. Trust me the bar cannot be set lower."[25] She also said: "The worst kind of bros are just self-centered douchebags that are trying to sell you shit in an MLM scheme while taking thirst trap pictures of their abs and posting them next to a clickbait hook."[26] She's my kind of girl!

Control access to create connection (and save your sanity)

Here's a groundbreaking revelation: being always on, everywhere, for anyone, is quite possibly the fastest way to go bonkers. Trust me. I've dabbled in a variety of methods for losing my marbles, and this one's a winner.

The only ones celebrating when we tumble headfirst into this "omnipresence trap" are the platform bosses, gleefully rubbing their hands as we pump our life force into their digital domains. And when we promise clients 24/7 accessibility, a lightning-fast 30 millisecond email response, daily social media miracles, all lovingly handcrafted by yours truly, our clients must think we're completely detached from reality. Because, honestly, who are we kidding here?

If you're nodding along, you've probably been there, done that and got the T-shirt. And if you haven't yet, well, consider this a friendly warning from the other side: omnipresence is overrated, and sanity is quite nice to hang onto.

We need to get rid of the thought that we need to be everywhere for everyone all at once. Byron Katie, in her book *Loving What Is*, asks a great question: "Who would you be without that thought?"[27] Take a moment and ask yourself that question. Who would you be without the thought that you had to be present on social media? Might it start to feel "social" again?

I've been running my own businesses for a while (nearly thirty years, can you believe it? BIFLXT[28]) and I've tried a lot of different things to grow my business: I've tried shouting, I've tried doing more, I've tried doing everything.

Maybe you've tried these things too? I've worked out that: I can't shout louder than everyone (I'm too short; nobody hears me from down here), I can't do more than 100% (that's what leads to burn out, Campari and bad maths), and I can't do everything (I'm really not that good, even though I have tricked myself into believing my own BS in the past).

So, what do you do?

I *can* create an intimate space, where members get heard; I don't have to do more or everything. So together we can get things done to grow our influence and businesses. That's what I've always done best – made safe, creative spaces for my clients to do their best thinking so they can make valuable things. **It's time to invite your favourite people to your**

dinner tables. Well, it might be breakfast where you are, but snacks are definitely encouraged.

Sharon Gaskin created Trainer Talk[29] to fill her own need – a safe place to discuss the business of training. She created a "table" where trainers can talk, discuss, get feedback and help, and collaborate. Sharon elevates members, giving them more opportunities to put themselves in the spotlight. To help trainers she created courses, events, local chapters, a matchmaking service and coaching. She is the epitome of the trainers' trainer, the top slot on The Asset Path. She has built trust and disrupted a sleepy industry. She is always innovating to avoid the apathy trap, listening to her membership, connecting deeply and frequently, and creating to fill their needs.

My personal mantra is: Always be adding value.

So if you're not going to be omnipresent what do we do to make sure when our potential clients have a need that we can fill they think of us?

We create top of mind awareness for the problem our potential clients have, and we do that by cultivating deep connections, thinking of people as special individuals and not target groups, being relevant and resonant, working on our product (that's probably us, our books, our services and events) so that they are so good we don't need advertising, and giving value generously. We need to be curious and courageous, as Dr Joanne Irving says in her book, *The C^2 Factor for Leadership*.[30] Curious to be truly interested in real people and courageous to give them more valuable resources and information than they expected.

This is how we demonstrate our credibility. This is how we increase trust and desirability.

Scale of connection

When trust and desire are high it's easier to get paid what we're worth, because clients accept and expect to pay for value.

Remember, not all connections are created equal. Let's break it down:

1. **Surface Connection**: The digital equivalent of nodding at someone in the street – polite but hardly profound. Question is, are you content with just skimming the surface, or are you itching to dive deeper?

2. **Engagement Connection**: This is where you actually engage (shocking, I know). Forget the fly-by 'nice post' comments. I'm talking about meaningful, thoughtful interactions. It's the difference between a mechanical handshake and a warm, solid grip that says, "I see you, mate." How often do you find yourself in these richer dialogues?

3. **Personal Connection**: Welcome to the inner circle, where connections transition from 'I know of you' to 'I understand you.' This is personal, like handwritten letter personal. These are the folks you DM at odd hours, share inside jokes with, and actually remember their birthdays (without Facebook reminders!). Reflect for a moment – how many do you

have in your corner?

4. **Trusted Connection**: Here lies mutual respect, unwavering trust and the kind of support that could hold up a bridge. These are your ride-or-die folks, your brainstorm buddies, your 4 a.m. crisis call. These connections are rare, but worth it. Who are your trusted confidantes?

5. **Transformational Connection**: The summit of connection Everest. These relationships change you, propel you, transform you from the caterpillar into the proverbial butterfly. They're not just part of your network; they're part of your growth, your journey, your story. Ever met someone who sparked a revolution in your life? That's what we're aiming for.

We want to be significant to other people. And they want to be significant to us.

You don't need to transform every nod into a soul-deep connection. But imagine, just imagine if you could turn even a handful of surface scratches into deep, meaningful bonds. What could that do for your credibility, your happiness, your sanity?

So, here's your homework: evaluate your current connections. How deep do your connections really go? Are you stuck at the surface, or are you ready to dive into the deep end?

In this world of infinite reach, we're aiming for infinite depth. Let's not just make connections; let's make them count.

Author and social scientist Sherry Turkle wrote the book, *Alone Together: Why We Expect More from Technology and Less from Each Other*[31] in 2011. Over a decade later it's more true than ever. We live in a technologically connected world while yearning for human connection. In the last ten years so much has changed, and so little.

> **The dark side of connection** lies in the frantic collection of likes and followers, going wide instead of deep, counting the wrong metrics.

3DQ: Connection

Think about these three directionally-correct questions:

1. How do I prove I am me? Deepfakes, copy cats and AI will churn out content at an incredible rate. Every time you appear in the world (written, audio, video) consider how you will demonstrate you are a real human?

2. Get off social. Where else are the people I want to connect with hanging out?

3. What do I really stand for? Why should people follow my flag?

---

1. Swift, Taylor. Quoted by Jeremy Waite. LinkedIn post. Accessed January, 2024 https://www.linkedin.com/posts/jeremypaulwaite_my-career-is-just-one-long-conversation-activity-7141056213106036738-obki

2. Some people call me a crazy cat lady because I have more than twenty cats. I agree.

3. Bezos, you know, the Amazon guy.

4. O'Leary, the chap that runs the airline that starts with an R (I'm not going to give them more business).

5. Tony Robbins, not God.

6. This reminds me of a joke I used to play on people turning up late to my events, ask me about it sometime and I'll tell you the full story.

7. The New Gurus, Helen Lewis: https://www.bbc.co.uk/programmes/p0dnlp6t

8. Epictetus. "Discourses I, 21.4."

9. Yes, all my clients are my favourite, but Emma has proven to have a particular affinity to my style of crazy!

10. Williams, E, *Leaving Academia: Ditch the blanket, take the skills*, 2024, Intellectual Perspective Press.

11. Jay Acunzo, https://jayacunzo.com/

12. Phil is the Co-CEO and Chief Mentor of 25eight in Australia, a certified B Corp that educates, coaches and mentors leaders who know it's time to grow their business, but need help to reach their goals.

13. Despite what Maybelline, BMW and Campari would have you believe.

14. You can get a copy of the Thought Leadership Canvas from www.thecredibilitycrisis.com

15. Reid Hoffman, the American venture capitalist and co-founder of LinkedIn. I don't think he programs the algorithms himself; he's probably got a few helpers.

16. *This Is Spinal Tap* is a mockumentary from the '80s, showcasing a fictional band with a rather unique amplifier that, unlike standard amps that peak at 10, goes to 11. I rely heavily on their concept of going to 11 which is why I've mentioned it so many times in this book.

17. I was also ruminating. AI is exciting and offers plenty of opportunity, in the right hands.

18. I lived in a cave in Spain for a while, before I did my fabulous midlife crisis. Not to get away from the world, but to get back to the real world.

19. The original concept of a "robot" as defined by Karel Čapek in *R.U.R. (Rossum's Universal Robots)* – essentially beings created for forced labour, lacking individuality and autonomy. Sounds like anyone you know?

20. *Your Truth Shared* podcast by Finola Howard: https://www.finolahoward.com/podcasts/your-truth-shared/episodes/2147846270

21. I hope I've just put the *X Files* opening notes into your head. They'll stay with you for the rest of the day. You're welcome.

22. Wilks, Corey, Psy.D. - Clinical Psychologist & Performance Coach. Accessed January, 2024. https://coreywilkspsyd.com/

23. I know I'm over-egging the metaphor. I was a teenager from a poor family, at an inner-city school who didn't smoke or cut classes. This was one of my few rebellions, don't knock it!

24. Louis Grenier interviews fascinating people who are doing disruptive things that add value. It's the only podcast for people sick of marketing bullshit. https://podcast.everyonehatesmarketers.com/

25. Louis Grenier | Everyone Hates Marketers | No-BS Marketing & Brand Strategy Podcast https://podcast.everyonehatesmarketers.com/episodes/how-to-build-an-authentic-social-presence-without-sounding-like-a-bro December 2023.

26. Find out more about Erica here https://www.ericaschneider.me/

27. Katie, Byron. *Loving What Is: Four Questions That Can Change Your Life*. Harmony, 2002.

28. BIFLXT – Before Instagram, Facebook, LinkedIn, X (formerly known as Twitter), TikTok. Difficult to imagine – we used to get business the hard way!

29. https://thetrainerstrainingcompany.co.uk/trainer-talk-membership/

30. Irving, Joanne, Ph.D. *The C² Factor for Leadership: How the Alchemy of Curiosity and Courage Helps Leaders Become Champions and Lead Meaningful Lives*. 1st ed., Routledge Productivity Press, 2022.

31. Turkle, Sherry. *Alone Together: Why We Expect More from Technology and Less from Each Other*. Basic Books, 2011.

SYNTHESIS

The Trust/Desire paradox

We can race around, disrupting all over the place, but if we never help a client get that transformation, they won't trust us. If our creations never solve a real problem, we won't be desirable. Without trust and desire we won't make connections (unless you're looking for one night stands!)

The paradox lies in balancing the disruption of creating new, exciting things (which grows desire) with the reliability and trustworthiness that come from consistency and proven results (which creates trust). It's about recognising that both trust and desire are essential for sustainable business growth and connections, and finding the right mix of innovation and dependability to occupy the High Desire/High Trust quadrant – The Credibility Quadrant.

Let's look what we can learn from the other quadrants.

Bro Comms: Dan Peña, perhaps the most Bro Comms bro out there, looks like he'd sit firmly in the top left – high desire and low trust.[1] His style is aggressive, angry, brash, critical and confrontational. He's known for his profanity,[2] which is both admired and criticised. His style is a stark (and dare I say hilarious) contrast to more conventional, softer approaches in the world of business coaching and personal development. Peña's style is unmistakable and polarising, making him a distinct figure in the world of business coaching.

I've had the interesting task of interviewing a couple of Peña's acolytes over the years;[3] guys who have followed the exact training of the self-named "50 Billion Dollar Man". One notable bro had a larger-than-life portrait of himself behind him during all our interviews.

His followers trust him implicitly, until they don't.

In *The Trusted Advisor* Maister, Green and Galford (sounds like a law firm) propose a formula that attempts to quantify the elements of trustworthiness.[4] A noble task! It's particularly relevant in professional relationships, such as between a consultant and a client, but can be applied in a broader context as well. *The Trusted Advisor* equation:

$$Trustworthiness = \frac{Credibility + Reliability + Intimacy}{Self\text{-}Orientation}$$

Their terms:

- Credibility: In a business context, credibility comes from being knowledgeable and offering good advice. It's about the expertise and skills you bring to the table.

- Reliability: This is about following through on actions and commitments, consistently meeting expectations. It's about dependability over time.

- Intimacy: The level of emotional safety, the ability to share confidential information, knowing it will be respected and kept secure. It's about the depth of the relationship.

- Self-Orientation: Where's the focus or motivation? On themselves or on others. High self-orientation (focus on yourself) diminishes trust, while low self-orientation (focus on the other person's interests and needs) enhances it.

The equation suggests that building trust involves not just increasing credibility, reliability and intimacy, **but also reducing self-orientation**. The more it looks like you are doing something for others rather than for yourself, the more trust you earn.

And this is where our Bro Comm-ers fall down. It's all about them. Yes, they will get attention, clients, money! But as their followers realise the shallowness of the relationship they will reciprocate. In the Bro Comm area you'll find the most copying, stealing and cheating. Everyone is out for themselves. There are a few intrepid souls who call the Bro Comm-ers out. I'm a fan of Mike Winnet, who did a series of videos exposing CONtrepreneurs[5] and Stephen Findeisen, better known as Coffeezilla who uncovers scams, fraudsters and fake gurus that are preying on desperate people with deceptive advertising.[6]

But the thing about Bro Comm-ers is they are onto something useful, and we shouldn't dismiss them without some investigation. We need to get attention, and they know how to do it. That larger-than-life-size portrait has kept the guy in my mind all these years – for the wrong reasons (natch!) – but at least I remember him.

It reminds me of a scene from *The Pirates of the Caribbean*, where James Norrington says: "You are without a doubt the worst pirate I've ever heard of."

And, Jack Sparrow replies: "But you have heard of me."[7]

Bore Comms: These are companies and people with high trust and low desirability. You've seen them. The website that says: "I'm a trusted advisor." The LinkedIn post that makes an "offer": "I do executive coaching." The book that claims: "Let's build a strong foundation." YES! We want all of those things, and we love and trust you, but we've heard it all before. We wouldn't be able to pick you out of a line-up of the usual suspects; Keyser Söze is safe.

The problem with bore comms is that it feels safe.

But you're unlikely to bore somebody into doing business with you.

Base camp: This bottom corner is just for you. Low desire (you don't have an offer) and low trust (you have no experience or qualifications in this area). You're not trying to impress anyone. You're talking into the void, a stream of consciousness type conversation with anyone and no one. This is where most new ideas start. In the inception point, where you have no credibility at all. It's a liberating space, rather than negative. If you're not trying to be desirable, and you don't need to be trusted you can experiment freely. This corner is dedicated to ideas, projects or concepts that are in their initial, formative stages. It's the beginning of a credibility journey or the embryonic stage of developing trustworthiness and authority in a particular field.

Nobody is expecting much from you here. It's an exciting freedom. You have plenty of room for growth and learning. But the biggest problem is a lack of direction. Without the external expectation it can be easy to get stuck here. This is where stagnation can occur if you're not pushed out of the comfortable base camp and forced to choose a mountain. Use the Old Co/New Co idea from the disruption chapter to get you moving.

This is a very simplified version of the Trust/Desire paradox. We all know there's more subtlety to it than this. My client Dan Kowalski cautions against the oversimplification of 2x2s in his book W.I.S.E Choices at Work: "The 2x2 creates a false comfort zone and encourages automatic thinking."[8] He goes further in his book to turn that messy middle into a danger zone.

Here's how that looks on our model. The apathy zone is where we are in danger of complacency or stagnation. Of believing our own BS.

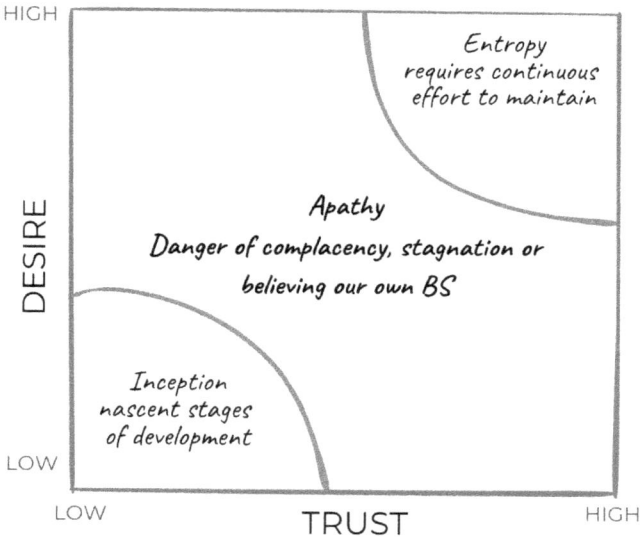

But the danger doesn't stop there. If you're in that coveted top slot with high trust and high desire, you're going to get hit with entropy! Remember we talked about hysteresis and entropy back in the Creation section?[9] Now you can see where it lives in our paradox.

Entropy is the biggest cause of the credibility crisis. Credibility is created over time, and decays with time. Entropy, in its most general scientific sense, is a measure of disorder or randomness in a system. Think of it as a natural tendency towards chaos over time (or is that a description of me?)

Your credibility can be subject to a kind of "entropy" if not maintained. You create a high level of credibility through consistent actions or quality services, solving the most important problems. But, without continual reinforcement, this credibility can erode. Missteps, lack of connection or failing to stay current can lead to a gradual decline in perceived reliability and reputation killing trust.

Trust also experiences a similar entropy. It's built slowly over time through consistent, reliable interactions. However, it can dissipate quickly if these trust-growing behaviours stop. Like energy in a closed system, the "trust energy" becomes less available to the system – in this case, the connection – if not replenished through ongoing trustworthy actions.

Initially, a product or idea may generate significant interest and desire. Without innovation, continued connection and disruption, this interest can decrease. Desire becomes dispersed, moving onto newer, more engaging offerings. Creation without connection to the needs of the people you serve you will pop you back into Base camp.

> Consistency in the right actions compounds over time. If you show up, defend the flag, create deep connections, demonstrate trustworthy actions, respond to disruption in measured and inspiring ways you will stop the credibility crisis.

The "entropy" effect highlights the need for continuous effort and adaptation. Just as energy must be input into a system to reduce entropy in physics, ongoing effort is required in business and relationships to maintain credibility, trust and desire.

Trust in yourself first

Joanne Irving (who wrote the book, *The C² Factor for Leadership*) says: "To be more courageous you need to see and own courage. Name the thing you see and you'll become it."

Her sentiment is echoed by Sheryl Sandberg:[10] "We cannot change what we are not aware of, and once we are aware, we cannot help but change."

For the last few years I've started to be brave again. I used to be "dangerous", as I mentioned earlier. Going back to being dangerous didn't feel right, but going forwards to being *more* daring does. I am daring. I claim it for myself, and look for opportunities to be daring. I had fallen into the apathy zone for too long, limping along with jobbing. I needed to disrupt myself.

In 2022, I started thinking about ways I could help more people go through my coaching program and get their books written. I was doing one-to-one, I love it, but its time intensive and therefore expensive. I wanted a better way to make my proven program accessible. We all know that information alone (course, book, articles) isn't enough. We need accountability, feedback, fun, a sense of being in it together. A cohort. I've now (end of 2023) led people through four cohorts, and the model is changing again for 2024 due to feedback (remember our Launch, Learn, Loop model).

I took a leap, again, to trust in myself and launch something new and disruptive.

Author and consultant, Jonathan Stark recently asked:[11]

"Does it make you mad when someone who's not as good as you gets better gigs simply because they're famous? Here's the thing...

1. Fame leads to trust

2. Trust leads to sales

So you can grumble about how unfair life is. Or you can take steps to be more famous."

The middle of that conundrum is trust.

Fame can be a significant factor in elevating trust. People often equate fame with credibility and reliability. Fame creates a perception of authority and expertise. **So you can complain, or you can get more famous.**

But what is trust? Can you manufacture or engineer it? Is it the same as authority? Can't I just write a book and create authority? We could have a really interesting conversation on the semantics; I'm sure it would be fun over a glass of something refreshing and cold. Authority is earned and position-based (think of people in authority), and credibility is being trusted through competence. Authority often stems from a position, a role or expertise, granting the power or right to give orders, make decisions or enforce obedience. **Credibility, on the other hand, is the quality of being trusted or believed in**, often earned over time through consistent integrity, honesty and competency.

While authority can be appointed or assumed, credibility is earned and can significantly enhance authority. In my world, **authority is about position, while credibility is about trustworthiness.**

Matt Church from Thought Leaders, says: "We teach that the commercially successful path requires you to first be relevant to a market, then thorough, then elegant before you start to focus on being unique."[12] Going for disruption (unique) is foolish if you don't have relevancy, experience and expertise, and an elegantly packaged creation.

Trust is about what you say and what you do.

You create trust by adding value to every connection, interaction and opportunity. More value than was expected, because:

Trust is about what other people say about what you say and what you do.

My nosey side has always been struck by Jeff Bezos's idea (founder of Amazon): "Your brand is what people say about you when you're not in the room." I've taken to asking my clients, rather than guessing!

It's straightforward really – the more authentically you connect with your clients, the more they trust you. It's not about schmoozing; it's about genuine engagement, listening and understanding their needs. This is the kind of trust that turns a one-off client into a lifelong advocate.

Create desire by being desirable

My mate Jeff also said: "A brand for a company is like a reputation for a person. You earn reputation by trying to do hard things well."[13]

Bezos was spot on when he likened a company's brand to a person's reputation, earned by doing the hard things well. This is where disruption comes into play. It's not about being different for the sake of it; it's about being boldly innovative, offering something that's not just new, but also desired. When you disrupt the norm in a way that hits the mark, you don't just get heads turning, you get hearts racing. That's the kind of desire we're talking about – one that keeps your clients coming back for more.

In *Wanting: The Power of Mimetic Desire in Everyday Life*, Luke Burgis[14] delves into René Girard's concept of mimetic desire, which suggests that human desires are not entirely individual or innate, but are largely imitated from others. You can transform mimetic desire as a force for good by consciously choosing positive models that inspire trust and authentic connection.

This is a proactive approach in which you embody the qualities, expertise and values that your target audience finds attractive or compelling. You need to become the person who naturally draws interest and desire. You might think of this as becoming a Key Person of Influence, as Daniel Priestley[15] says in the book of the same name. The book argues that being a key person of influence allows you to shape your industry rather than just compete within it, leveraging your expertise and network to create more significant impact and achieve greater success.

It's not about "personal branding" or projecting an image. It's about having a clear and defended flag that creates a solid foundation of desire. When people know exactly what you stand for, it creates a sense of reliability and authenticity. This creates a deeper connection and desire among the audience to engage with what you're offering. Then people will want to follow the flag. **Be the flag bearer, not the flag.**

Also remember that Jay Acunzo talks about "resonance". I'm an engineer, so resonance, in the physical world, is about finding that perfect frequency where everything just clicks, where the output is effortlessly amplified. In our world, it's about hitting that sweet spot where what we offer vibrates perfectly with what our audience craves. **It's not about shouting louder; it's about speaking the language that echoes in the hearts and minds of those we seek to serve.**

Imagine trying to force a tuning fork to resonate at a frequency it's not designed for. The result? Discord, not harmony. Similarly, in our business relationships and communications, attempting to manufacture desire or resonance can lead to dissonance with our audience. It's like wearing shoes that don't fit; no matter how hard you try, you'll never be comfortable.

Desperation shouts. Expertise whispers.

Forcing desire is like building a house on quicksand instead of solid ground. It might stand for a moment, but it lacks stability and authenticity, and eventually, it will sink. True desire can't be fabricated through high-pressure tactics or flashy gimmicks. It's born from authenticity, from understanding and aligning with the genuine needs and values of the people you want to reach.

The irony of trying to force these elements is that it often leads to the opposite of what we desire. Instead of attracting, we repel. Instead of growing trust, we erode it. The key is to focus on cultivating an environment where desire can grow naturally. This approach may require patience, but it is the only way to ensure that the connection we make is not only strong but lasting.

By harnessing mimetic desire, you can create a ripple effect of trust and authentic credibility, effectively countering the credibility crisis. When you make your path through business (and life) visible to others you are creating the desire path for others to follow.

Solving the paradox

Green's Trust Equation can be integrated with our three dials of Disruption, Creation, and Connection:

1. Disruption: Challenges norms, with the emphasis on reducing "self"-orientation, encouraging innovation and new perspectives.

2. Creation: Aligns with credibility and reliability in the Trust Equation. Creation involves developing competent, reliable solutions or content, enhancing your credibility.

3. Connection: Mirrors intimacy in the Trust Equation. Fostering genuine connections boosts trust. Connection can be likened to how intimacy in the equation represents emotional safety and empathy.

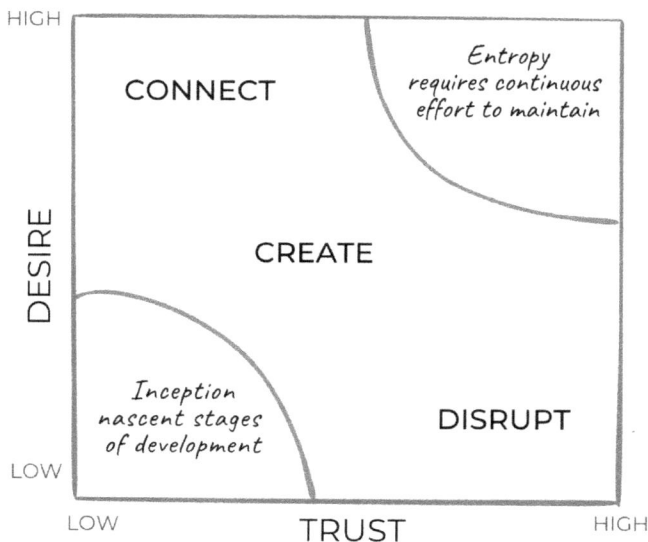

To counter the Bro Comm-ers' bragging problem, just add connection.

To fix being boring, Bore Comm-ers get a bit disruptive.

To balance the system, add creation of valuable assets.

So, should we turn the dials up to 11 on all three of these dimensions? Do we want high disruption? Clearly, no. Should we be aiming for an 11 on the creation scale? Only if we want to compete head on with the AI jockeys and content farms, or never get to completion on The Asset Path. Do we want really high connection? This is the trickiest to answer, and I've always been an 11 type of girl. Until recently. To go deep we can't go wide. Society is measuring and rewarding for wide (you've been keeping score of your followers too). Business, especially for thought leaders and consultants, is done with the deep connections that come from referrals. I propose a curated connection strategy. Aim for a wide influence within a deep niche. What does this look like?

Desired disruption

In *Same as Ever: A Guide to What Never Changes*, Morgan Housel says: "We are very good at predicting the future, except for the surprises—which tend to be all that matter."[16]

It's those surprises that will get us every time. To reduce their disruptive force, and give us back some semblance of control, we can protect our core and disrupt at the edges (the old co / new co model from earlier). You already have success, clients, contacts, experience. Don't uproot the tree while reaching for new fruit.

When I moved to Spain in 2005, desperate to get more connected with nature, I was most excited about the number of trees I had, and in planting more. David the elder,[17] my slippered neighbour, would show me his trees. He was most excited about a plum tree, that his father (David) had planted years before during the civil war. David the elder (not David the elder elder) had carefully grafted a white plum scion onto one branch. In late summer, the intense pink flowers gave way to a bipolar display of black plums on one half and white on the other. The well-established root system of the original tree allowed the graft to take, and grow, combining the best characteristics of the two.

This is the magic of growing from what's already stable and strong.

Constrained creation

Don't flood your market with services, products, ways to work with you, options, new things every day. We must get well-acquainted with constraints. Think about your year in quarters or seasons. Deliver a new or upcycled valuable asset per season. Then cultivate connections and capitalise on the asset you created. Get through the launch, learn, loop framework fast and consistently. Upcycle your sawdust, the offcuts and "waste" from your creations. One person's waste is another's gold. Track and stack assets, lead people on an asset journey not a treasure hunt.[18]

Creation = Curiosity + Constraints

If you don't name, claim and create your idea into a way for us mere mortals to consume it, you are not a thought leader. You're a thinker. You sit firmly in the bottom left – no trust and no desire. It's easy for brilliant people to get out of that corner with constrained creation.

Curated connection

In *Belonging to the Brand: Why Community is the Last Great Marketing Strategy*, Mark Schaefer, futurist and the bestselling author says: "The world is in a belonging crisis and those who can bring people together in community can create a deep and lasting emotional connection ... which of course is the goal of your brand."[19]

Be most relevant and resonant (to use Jay Acunzo's beautiful word) with those people you can help.

Restrict access to go deeper. Encourage referrals by being the most valuable resource to a special group of insiders.

Curated connection is about bringing people together around your brand. Mckinsey say we've moved from mass media, through personalisation into community, going from marketing for reach, solving for effectiveness to now influencing.[20] We influence through building trust and having a desirable solution to the most important problem for our special group of insiders.

You don't have to be everyone's friend. And nobody wants a false friend. You can stand out and take sides.

Desire must be rooted in the solid ground of authenticity. It's about being genuinely in tune with our values, our expertise and the needs of those we aim to help. When these elements align, our message doesn't just reach our audience; it resonates, creating a powerful, lasting harmony.

This is how desire is ignited and sustained – not through flash-in-the-pan tactics, but through a consistent, resonant frequency that draws people in and keeps them close. We find ourselves not just standing on solid ground, but turning it into a magnet that attracts and holds the very people we're meant to serve.

Invest all your energy in understanding, listening, looping, creating for your one client. Make them feel special and desired. Then you will be desirable. I fall in love with all my clients (yes, even you, Jim![21]); I tell them this at the end of our calls.

> Yeats: "There are no strangers here; only friends you haven't yet met."
> Debs: "There are no strangers, only clients you haven't met yet!"
> Debs' mom: "Stop talking to strangers!"

As an established expertise-based business owner, you know that the balance between trust and desire is important. If you've got trust down pat, your clients know you're the real deal. They respect your expertise. But if there's no desire? Well, that's like having a loyal audience who applauds politely but never rushes to the stage for an encore (or an *"otra"* as we say in Spain). You're appreciated, sure, but are you really shaking things up and keeping them hooked?

Now, let's flip it. Imagine you've stirred up plenty of desire. There's buzz, excitement, the works. But if trust isn't part of the mix, it's like a hit pop song: catchy at first, but forgotten by next week. Your clients might be initially intrigued, but without that solid ground of trust, they're not sticking around for the second album.

We need to keep blending trust with a continuous stream of desire. It's about being not just relevant, but irresistible. That go-to expert who not only knows their stuff but also keeps clients on the edge of their seats, eager for what's next.

Please take 5 minutes to leave me a review, it helps other people to decide if they want to read the book, and I'll be eternally grateful. If you're reading on Kindle just scroll to the end of the book. If you're reading the paperback, please go to your favourite bookstore.

Remember, you can get the promised downloads at www.shortvaluablebooks.com or scan the QR code.

---

1. There are probably some female Bro Comm-ers; I just don't know any.

2. I'm not against swearing, though I didn't swear until I was 28 years old. It was part of my "running your own business" education. Now I'm an expert swearer in three languages.

3. I chose this word carefully; it really is like the Church of Peña.

4. An oldie, but a goodie. Maister, David H., Charles H. Green, and Robert M. Galford. *The Trusted Advisor*, 2000, Free Press

5. Watch some of Mike's videos here: http://www.youtube.com/@MikeWinnet

6. Don't go down the rabbit hole, you've been warned! Coffeezilla: https://www.youtube.com/@Coffeezilla

7. *The Pirates of the Caribbean* is a funtabulous swashbuckler film series starting in 2003.

8. Dan Kowalski, *W.I.S.E. Choices at Work: Go from doubting to DECISIVE when the clock is ticking*, 2023, Intellectual Perspective Press

9. Apathy and entropy? It sounds like a heavy metal band from the '80s. No wonder we're exhausted.

10. Sandberg, Sheryl. *Lean In: Women, Work, and the Will to Lead.* Knopf, 2013.

11. He does a great comic strip for consultants, called Ditcherville: https://jonathanstark.com/ditcherville/

12. Thought Leaders, https://thoughtleaders.com.au/ Church, Matt, Peter Cook, and Scott Stein. *The Thought Leaders Practice. 1st ed.*, Thought Leaders Global, 2016.

13. Bezos again, not Jeff down the pub.

14. Burgis, Luke. *Wanting: The Power of Mimetic Desire in Everyday Life.* St. Martin's Press, 2021.

15. Priestley, Daniel. *Key Person of Influence: The Five-Step Method to Become One of the Most Highly Valued and Highly Paid People in Your Industry.* Rethink Press, 2014.

16. M. Housel, *Same as Ever: A Guide to What Never Changes,* 2023, Portfolio.

17. Not to be confused with David the son, or David the grandson. I wonder when he became "the elder"?

18. That's a note to myself, I am the worst for creating assets and scattering them, hoping people will find them! Make it easy.

19. M. Schaefer, *Belonging to the Brand: Why Community is the Last Great Marketing Strategy*, 2022, Schaefer Marketing Solutions

20. *A better way to build a brand: The community flywheel*, September 28, 2022, https://www.mckinsey.com/capabilities/growth-marketing-and-sales/our-in sights/a-better-way-to-build-a-brand-the-community-flywheel

21. Jim's name has been changed to protect the innocent, but they know who they are!

The real antidote

The reason why the credibility crisis feels so strong now is because, if you're like me, it feels like time is accelerating.[1] You're getting one day closer to death,[2] the desire path ahead is probably shorter than the one you've travelled, and you might even be thinking of one last hurrah! If you're on the other end of the timescale, the future probably looks really blurry: you can't see the mountain, the online noise is deafening, you're encouraged to follow the same old routes, but nobody is interested in showing you the directions.

The real antidote to the credibility crisis comes down to these three profitable strategies, and when you learn to love them, you'll enjoy the journey even more, *and* win business:

1. **Desired Disruption** is the catalyst – be **daring and bold** in connecting with interesting people and thinking new thoughts to increase desire, while maintaining the solid ground you have.

2. **Constrained Creation** is the currency – show your expertise through writing a series of **transformative** books, creating **innovative** content, being featured in industry-leading journals, and delivering **powerful** speeches.

3. **Curated Connection** is the cure – cultivate **trust** with one-on-one connections, personal interactions and direct engagement through live events, coaching sessions and interactive platforms.

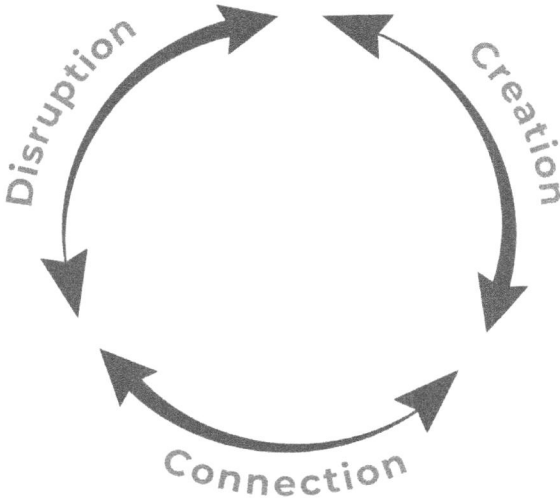

Yes, we will use all the tools at our disposal and take advantage of AI and automation, we'll outsource and delegate, be agile and disrupt ourselves. We'll move quickly when needed while protecting the core of our business. And we'll rest without losing solid ground, watching for the signals ready to move. We'll look back now and then to be sure the people we're connecting with are still following, and we'll look up to make sure we're still heading in the right direction. We won't be surprised by fake flag bearers, false peaks and fabricated stories. **We might zig when others are zagging and be daring even though we're afraid.**

The credibility crisis will reach a saturation point.

Genuine experts will adopt more visible methods to demonstrate their expertise. There will be a clear divide. On one side, experts with verified credentials and on the other, the "pop-up" experts whose credibility fades as quickly as it appeared.

If we're not careful, the next generation might grow cynical, disbelieving everything and everyone, leading to a society that's perpetually sceptical. Remember the Y2K scare? Imagine that level of panic, but with every piece of advice or information we receive. Chaos, indeed, but not the good kind.

The credibility crisis is not just a fleeting trend; it's a reflection of our times. But with awareness and an emphasis on genuine credibility, we can find solid ground. Your credibility is more than a personal attribute. When misinformation is rampant, being a source of reliable and honest information is crucial. Your commitment to truth, transparency and integrity doesn't just benefit you; it contributes to a foundation of trust and reliability that is sorely needed.

The key to growing credibility is not to conquer every hill, but to firmly and proudly stand by your flag. It's about depth over breadth, and authenticity over omnipresence. It's about standing firmly, with your flag, and saying, here I am. Are you clear about *your* flag?

This revolution is about shifting from seeking immediate gains, likes and follows, and sharing a surface-level image to aiming for lasting influence and deep respect. It's about valuing real understanding over quick judgements in a divided world. Your credible approach can spark change and foster meaningful discussions. Whether as a consultant, business leader or team member, your influence matters. By consistently displaying your core values and expertise, you help create a more informed, rational and understanding society.

Listen, there's a credibility crisis, and it's your fault. Which means you can fix it. You need to find your disruptive idea, create valuable assets and connect deeply. Simple.

We seek change because of disruption; we remain the same because of apathy.

Everything is downstream of connection.

Creation is how you break the brain   world barrier.

Disruption comes last.

Be daring, darling.[3]

---

1. I know it isn't, time doesn't exist!

2. Nod to Pink Floyd's *Time* lyrics, not a threat!

3. And for my final endnote, a quick reminder from one of my favourite series, *Blackadder Goes Forth*, where General Melchett says to Captains Darling and Blackadder: "If nothing else works, a total pig-headed unwillingness to look facts in the face will see us through."

Epilogue

I get to start again.

Disruption has given me a new chance.

In one day I can create an offer, test it and modify it – using a virtual team, AI and automations.

I can reach anyone across the world, within a few degrees of separation. And frequently they'll take a call with me.

I can whip up a website, design a brochure, hire an assistant and sit back and admire the view at the Disaster Farm.

I do not need permission.

I do not need deep pockets.

I do not need more degrees.

Not only that, but I have a wealth of knowledge, experience, failures *and* successes to back it up.

I am daring to be more me.

I am not playing it safe.

I am standing on solid ground.

Acknowledgements

Whenever the ground feels shaky for me there are a few people I call on to prop me up, and give me a hand while I ready myself. I look to others to show me what bravery and courage look like in the face of adversity. My girl gang: Karen Currier, Estelle Read, Carrie Eddins and Lisa de Caux.[1] They all help me in different ways so I can become more daring and, dare I say it, disruptive.

---

1. Really, this is my final endnote. I also call upon Stoic Steve, but he's imaginary and won't appreciate the name check.

Who is Debbie Jenkins?

As a kid, I devoured second hand, thumbed copies of the Bible, Isaac Asimov, the revised 13th edition of Encyclopedia Britannica (except PAS-PLA, missing in action) and the Reader's Digests. I knew I'd end up doing something with books, despite a careers advisor warning me against it.

The first publishing business I started in 2004, specialised in publishing unique non-fiction titles by genuine experts and thought leaders with niche books that, although mainstream publishers tend to overlook, were packed with information hungry readers wanted. At the heart of everything we did was fair play and efficiency. We worked hard to create a virtuous circle and put profit back into our authors' pockets while building a viable business ourselves. I exited that company in 2011, and they've gone on to do even greater things.

I love working with smart consultants, coaches and mentors who are brilliant at serving their clients, and also need to take care of their own practice. I've been running my own consultancy businesses for the last 25+ years. My first business was a digital marketing agency in the '90s helping consultants, coaches, trainers, speakers and expert advisors to grow their business while reducing marketing waste. Over the next three years I grew that company to 12 employees, an office in the city, a chillax room for the team... I thought I knew what I was doing. But I missed capitalising on a vital step – I didn't create enough assets that would work for me so that I didn't have to keep on selling my own and my team's time.

I know that it's easy to get caught up delivering to clients, keeping on top of trends and technology, marketing and proposal writing, racing from job to job. It's hard to squeeze in time for your own personal professional development, let alone find space to think about creating assets. And there's the dilemma, because without these assets you'll always be bouncing from job to job, selling your time not your value, and leaving your best ideas on your busy desk.

Over the last 25 years I have helped COOs from Microsoft, VPs from McDonald's and Executives from Mars (the company, not the planet) create, build and launch assets that have helped them win clients, build their personal practices and become published authors*. Through my publishing company I published over 80 business books.

After I sold it I went on to help more than 30 smart business owners write their legacy book, and coached hundreds of consultants to market themselves, their business, and their

IP. I have ghostwritten bestselling business books for venture capitalists, CFOs, MBEs, professors, mentors and coaches. I have designed and marketed apps, produced websites and written/co- written more than 20 books (my first in 2003). In the last few years, I have had coaching clients get published with Bloomsbury, Pearson, Business Expert Press, BIS, and Taylor & Francis. Other coaching clients chose themselves, decided the best route would be to use a hybrid publisher, or they've self-published. Each route to publishing is valid and has its own pros and cons. Now, I'm helping experts get their book written and published through my own publishing company, Intellectual Perspective Press.

I know how to help you get the clever ideas out of your head (or off your computer) and turned into valuable things (assets) for your business. Assets like business books, whitepapers, converting websites, marketing materials, podcasts … I also know how to help you use these assets to accelerate your time to impact, achieve visibility and influence, and improve your bottom line – that is The Asset Path.

I have a 1st Class Degree in Electronics Engineering which means I am trained to look for sustainable and innovative solutions to problems, I understand technology and software development, and I can create models and frameworks that people can use (and I know what a MOSFET is). I moved to Southern Spain in 2005. I live at the Disaster Farm (that's not a typo) with a host of animals, where I invite special clients to visit and work on their assets in person. I only work ten months of the year because the Disaster Farm needs my attention too – and if I don't take a break who's going to hand feed the horses juicy carrots and lounge around reading all those books I've bought?

I am determined to help all my clients make the most of their IP, ideas and talent. I can help you turn your clever ideas into valuable things. And we'll have fun doing it.

* I work with people from companies that don't start with an M too!

Other books by Debbie Jenkins

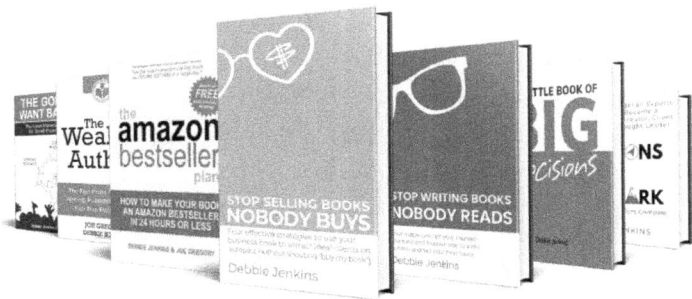

Get Debbie's other books at
www.ShortValuableBooks.com

Still not sure what to do?

I know I've thrown a lot of ideas at you in this book. Like I said at the start, I don't know all the answers. I wish I did. I'd share them with you, I promise. What I do know is that if anything in this book has piqued your interest, then come and join us at *Ideas into Assets*, our free bi weekly mastermind where we discuss all things thought leadership and creating valuable assets. www.debbiejenkins.com

The currency to stop The Credibility Crisis is creation

You may have noticed I think a well written, atomic business book is a valuable creation for smart experts. The first step in creating a business book as your minimum valuable asset is to join us for a Book Strategy Canvas session. You can get your copy and a video walkthrough from: www.thecredibilitycrisis.com

Your Book Strategy Canvas

Already an author or want to write a book?

I have a community of leaders who join me for regular strategy calls about writing and using their business books. Find out if this will be a fit for you: OnlyAuthors.club

Want to write a book as part of a cohort?

Write your next book with my team as part of a Publishing Cohort. We regularly start a new cohort of smart leaders and consultants, who are ready and prepared to get their valuable ideas tested, written and published. There's a waitlist, join us at: ExpertAuthor.academy

More Praise for Stop The Credibility Crisis

In 'Stop The Credibility Crisis', Debbie Jenkins invites us on an urgent quest to overcome the shadows of doubt cast by our limiting beliefs. Through her compelling narrative, she provides the tools to forge a path of disruption and creation, leading to undeniable credibility. **This book is a treasure for those ready to conquer their fears and step into the light of their true potential.**

Rachel Evers, Legal Counsel and Director of Legal Affairs, international Organisation for Migration, author of *Your Personal Quest,* https://rachelevers.com/

I thoroughly enjoyed Stop The Credibility Crisis. It was totally obvious from the beginning that a lot of thought had gone into this. It certainly wasn't a regurgitation of stuff from AI or other books. ***I loved these statements: "People buy transformation." "Disrupt to add value." "If you never create, that's not leadership, that's just thought."*** *And I loved the concept of desire paths. It was a useful book to stimulate thought and turn it into credibility. There is so much crap winging its way around the web because very few people can be bothered to create original thought. Apparently this takes up too much time and effort. But for those who can be bothered, they need this book to be able to bring themselves to the fore and make their thoughts shine!*

Alice Elliott - The Fairy Blogmother – https://fairyblogmother.co.uk/

As a trainer of 30 plus years experience, I recognise the landscape that Debbie Jenkins describes at the start of this book: the seismic changes in technology, the blurring of professional/personal boundaries and the constant disruption. This book offers a path for experienced consultants and thought leaders, not newbies. It is about creating, crafting and curating our own knowledge and expertise to give us a feeling of standing on solid ground. She offers us a solid practical strategy that acknowledges our humanity (moving through grief stages at time), offers antidotes to our objections and how to use trust as the bedrock of our business so that we are shining lighthouses in this chaotic landscape. The book is peppered with reflection questions to help apply her strategies to your business. This book is borne of the author's work with hundreds of writers and entrepreneurs to help craft what she calls "Minimum Valuable Assets" and to become trusted guides in this landscape. **If you are an experienced consultant/entrepreneur and feeling unsettled – buy this book. It won't settle you down but it will give you a light.**

Anne Walsh – The Excel Lady (author of 8 books and trainer of 30 plus years), www.the-excel-lady.com

I thoroughly recommend this book – particularly if, like me, you have been relying on telepathy as a marketing technique, and then wondering why "the newcomers are eating your lunch". Right from the get-go you can hear Debbie's giggle and sense of humour as she tells you the truth and leaves you reeling. The thing is, this book is not just about being warm and cuddly with catchy footnotes and obscure references to Mr Beast and Spinal Tap (I really am not cool enough), Debbie also brings the research, the diagrams, and the solid experience to make a real difference. This is a book about being daring and bold; about creating the right kind of content that is innovative, transformative and impactful; and cultivating real connection through personal interactions. **If you want to stop being boring with the same old same old offers, with no one buying what you have to sell, if you want to stop being quiet but not just be part of the rest of the noise, read this book!**

Joanna Denton, The Ridiculous Coach, https://joannadenton.com/

*How do expertise-based business owners not just survive but thrive in this whirlwind of change that is the prevailing economy? That's just the question **Debbie Jenkins** answers in her short yet powerful latest book, Stop The Credibility Crisis. **Stuffed full of valuable tips, techniques and masterful strategy, it's an MBA on how to stand out from the crowd!***

Sharon Eden - The Wild Elder - Spiritual Psychotherapist Coach,
https://thewildelder.com/

*'The Credibility Crisis' might be a short book. But don't expect to read it quickly. I found myself putting it down on practically every page as I pondered the concepts it put forward and the questions it proposed. **Debs has really brought the VUCA battle to life for those of us who are working to stand out in a very crowded world.** And she's also provided a strategy so you can face that battle fearlessly.*

David Pullan, Lead Alchemist at The Story Spotters and author of 'The DNA of
Engagement', https://thestoryspotters.com/

Almost 60 years ago, Nobel Laureate Bob Dylan wrote a song called "It' Alright, Ma (I'm Only Bleeding). In it he has a line "That he not busy being born is busy dying." He wrote this when mainframe computers took up tons of floor space and required massive cooling and other infrastructure. Only academics and large corporations had access. Today we carry more computing power in our pockets. With this acceleration of technology, Mr. Dylan could update his lyrics to say if we are not busy being born, then we are BUSIER dying. No need for this update because in "Stop the Credibility Crisis" Debbie Jenkins has covered this. Unlike Mr. Dylan, who only makes us wonder what to do, Ms. Jenkins provides several how-to techniques to confront the crisis in credibility we all face. (Yes, all of us!) Even if you work inside of a company, your credibility can be (or already is) in crisis. (For the record, Debbie says she has not written a how-to book, but she has put quite a lot of how after telling you why you should do something to up your credibility.)

Her three tenets of Disrupt, Create, Connect sound simple. Nevertheless, they require action, intentionality, and effort. (Perhaps Mr. Dylan knew it would take work to be 'busy' being born?) She provides great ideas for how to keep busy and become even more credible. If you need more reasons to read this book, the endnotes provide information and entertainment. Where else will you find references to Drucker, Epictetus, Emerson, AND the movie "This Is Spinal Tap"?

Dan Kowalski, Solution Instigator, author of *W.I.S.E. Choices At Work*, https://www.planathinking.com/

Anyone with expert or consultancy status would do well to read this before their next marketing investment. We all know that Social Media has re-written the script on buying, we can often see how real expertise is being replaced by gazillion-view teenage influencers. We even have senior politicians telling us: "people have had enough of experts". As if that's not enough, now we have the additional challenges of AI. And yes, you might be fondly thinking of the past – remembering the past "credible you", who could demonstrate wisdom based on years of knowledge, testimonials and experience. But now, you might be feeling your degrees, background, experiences are no longer needed? Did you just need a YouTube channel all along? So how do you find your clients? How does a serious buyer look for a credible advisor? What's happening to credibility? What do you, the expert, do – to prove your own?

Answer: We need experts more than ever to help find our way through the attention-grabbing, loud, sparkly, vacuous fall-out. Fortunately, Debs (in her inimitable style, with humour and self-deprecation, and a LOT of actual experience – despite her youthful looks she's no millennial!) has taken the nebulous and essential concept of Credibility and provided a flexible framework for the credibility crisis that we are now in.

Sue Haswell, Strategic Comms, https://suehaswell.co.uk/

www.ingramcontent.com/pod-product-compliance
Lightning Source LLC
Chambersburg PA
CBHW071420210326
41597CB00020B/3589